MasterWork

MASTERWORK

Arnaud Maitland

Dharma Publishing

SKILLFUL MEANS SERIES

Skillful Means
Mastering Successful Work

ISBN: 0-89800-309-1; 0-89800-310-5 (casebound)

With special thanks to Marcia Freedman, Hillary Powers, Dagmar Traub, Ron Spohn, Jack Petranker, Zara Wallace, and especially to Caroline van Tuyll van Serooskerken.

Printed and bound in the United States of America by Dharma Press, Berkeley, California.

9 8 7 6 5 4 3 2 1

Contents

To Rinpoche

Foreword

Early in the 1970s, having recently arrived in this country after ten years as a refugee in India, I founded Dharma Press, a company dedicated to printing and publishing the works of the Tibetan Buddhist tradition. I had already taught myself the basics of printing in India, but to succeed in the business environment of the United States required learning a whole new set of business skills, such as how to produce works of high quality, use time effectively, monitor finances, coordinate different phases of production, and communicate well with one another and with our suppliers.

I soon realized that Buddhist teachings offered numerous insights and guidance relevant to these concerns, and began to explore this connection in a systematic way. Students sometimes wrote down my informal talks on these topics, and these notes became the foundation for a shared body of knowledge we could all draw on. We were learning efficient and effective ways to do our work, while also developing our intelligence, energy, and decision-making skills.

As we learned the techniques necessary to do increasingly refined printing and operate more successfully as a business, we began to incorporate this knowledge into our lives. The foundation was appreciation for the importance of discipline and hard work to get the job done. Beyond that we had to develop such skills as using energy, time, and materials well and coping with shortages of space, conflicts in scheduling, and limited resources.

We found that we were most effective when we combined three fundamental practices: contemplation that always kept sight of the whole, awareness that kept track of all details and each step in the process, and fresh energy that we renewed every day. In 1978, I presented some of these basic lessons in a small book called *Skillful Means*. This work, which has since been adopted for classroom use in over a hundred colleges and universities, from junior colleges to graduate schools of business, has been translated into Dutch, German, French, Hungarian, Italian, Portuguese, and Spanish. Fifteen years later, a second volume about Skillful Means, known as *Mastering Successful Work,* followed.

The practice of Skillful Means proved helpful in all the organizations established under my guidance: the Nyingma Institute, which offered classes and residential programs based on teachings and practices of Buddhism; Odiyan, a new home for Buddhism in the West; and Dharma Publishing, where sales people as well as production staff made use of the same principles. We had also begun to do some commercial printing to generate revenue, and this meant applying

Skillful Means in a whole new range of activities, including estimating, marketing, and customer service. We had established centers in Europe and South America, and there too Skillful Means seemed to meet with a good response—not only in our centers, but also in the business community.

All of us at Dharma Press shared the fundamental goal of preserving the twelve-hundred-year-old tradition of Tibetan Buddhism, threatened with extinction through the subjugation of Tibet by a foreign power. Simply wishing that things were different was not enough; if we wanted to keep the teachings intact, we had to take decisive action. The practice of Skillful Means grew naturally out of that intention, for its methods gave us the key to accomplishing a great deal with very limited resources.

In 1981 we completed our first large-scale publishing venture: a complete reprint edition of the Tibetan Buddhist canon, containing the teachings of the Buddha and the commentaries of the great Indian masters. In Tibet the two parts of the canon consisted of about four hundred volumes, which we reprinted in 120 atlas-sized volumes, designed to last for centuries.

In 1997, after years of painstaking effort, we completed a far more ambitious project, known as Great Treasures of Ancient Teachings, which collected fundamental works of the Tibetan tradition in more than 620 volumes. During these years, we also published over a hundred titles in English, produced and distributed more than 180,000 volumes of texts to Tibetans in exile and in Tibet, and preserved over 700 authentic reproductions of sacred art, donating hundreds of thousands of copies to Buddhist practitioners in India, Nepal, and elsewhere.

Acting together, the Nyingma organizations have created a home in the West for the three aspects of enlightened being (kaya, vaca, and chitta): The mandala of Odiyan and over a hundred thousand statues of Padmasambhava, the founder of Buddhism in Tibet, represent kaya, the physical embodiment of the Buddha; the monumental publishing projects we have been privileged to complete represent vaca, the voice of the Buddha; and the Enlightenment Stupa of Odiyan, one of the most beautiful in the West, represents chitta, the enlightenment of the Buddha.

Each of these accomplishments required genuine effort from our small organizations. Often we managed to succeed at projects that experts had told us were impossible, and we noticed that people repeatedly seemed surprised at how much we had been able to do. These signs of success showed us that the Skillful Means approach really works. We got similar feedback from individuals who left our organizations and used what they had learned with us to build a successful professional career. Based on this feedback, and on the interest in the published materials, we began to offer Skillful Means classes and programs.

Over the years, I have personally been quite surprised at the impact of the Skillful Means teachings. After all, I came from a country where Western culture and Western ways of working were completely un-known. When I arrived in America, my early students thought that spirituality had to do with meditation, or perhaps with chanting and prayer, but they certainly did not imagine it had anything to do with finding satisfaction in hard work. We have had to make those connections for ourselves, through our own experience.

Today, however, there is no longer any room for doubt. Work is a way for human beings to cultivate the qualities of persistence, flexibility, and the courage to deal with challenges. Because it leads to tangible results, work provides useful feedback on one's own state of mind and understanding, and because it promotes success, it builds confidence in one's own abilities. All these factors count for just as much in the spiritual realm as they do in the everyday world of work.

The Skillful Means Attitude

In Buddhist texts, the word for 'means' or 'method' is 'upaya', and the word for 'skill', in the sense of knowledge or wisdom, is 'prajna'. These two terms are interactive; they suggest that possessing 'skillful means' means knowing how to use knowledge itself to achieve your goals. The tradition discusses both these terms on many levels, and it is almost impossible to capture their full meaning in English. Instead, I have focused on how 'means' and 'knowledge' manifest in the activity of working. In our Nyingma organizations, work has become an important way of practicing the teachings of Buddhism.

In Skillful Means, work is seen as a journey into unknown realms. The further you go, the more challenges you encounter. Dealing with these challenges allows you to accumulate important knowledge and develop fundamental skills. You can learn how events in the past gave rise to the present, how to analyze what is happening right now, and how to predict the quality of the future you are creating through your present action. At the same time you learn what to do to reach your goal. The whole process can be enjoyable and deeply rewarding.

Whether this is your outlook on work depends on whether you approach it with the right attitude. If you see work as an unavoidable duty, something unpleasant to be avoided whenever possible, work will end up controlling your life. If you work in order to obtain possessions with the money you earn, or for reasons of ego and status, you still will find little fulfillment in work itself. Even if you work out of a sense of obligation to do well—what is commonly viewed as the 'work ethic'— you will not be taking full advantage of the opportunities work offers.

If you see work as a journey toward fulfillment, however, then each challenge you master transforms who you are, automatically bringing abundance and a sense of well-being. Work becomes more like art: You work for the joy of working. You may not be able to say for certain whether you will succeed at whatever you do, but by giving your full effort, you create the possibility of producing something richly creative—unimaginable and unique.

This approach to work is the attitude that Skillful Means fosters. A Skillful Means attitude means starting each day, each project, each activity with a positive outlook, preparing for what needs to be done to bring about success. It means preparing for work the way an athlete prepares for an event or game, focusing on essentials and on letting energy flow freely. With that kind of attitude, you can easily apply your skills and talents to the task at hand, learn something new, and generate creative solutions to problems as they arise.

Anyone who develops a Skillful Means attitude will naturally become a leader, playing a key role in any enterprise. Whatever projects you take on will be charged with beauty, depth, purpose, and dynamic creativity. With a Skillful Means attitude, it is easy to inspire other people to do more, because you are getting results that look almost magical.

Of course, you know that the secret is in your control, and that anyone else could share the same secret, but that is not the way it looks to others. They want to know what you are doing that is special; how you are able to do what you do. They wish they could do the same: not just to get ahead or make a favorable impression, but because they can see that getting good results is a part of what makes work enjoyable and makes every day into an adventure. When several people in a business share this same attitude, the consequences are even more dramatic. Success follows on success, building the confidence to take on new challenges and accept greater risks for the sake of the guiding vision.

Success through Work

Buddhist teachings emphasize the quality of virya, which means vigor or discipline. In the practice of virya, mind and body interact in a way that promotes the virtue and discipline of each. Virtue has its own discipline, and discipline has its virtue. When you bring them together, you replace being fooled with finding fulfillment. Challenging your awareness and energy, perfecting your inner resources, you can be successful in any activity. When you have learned how to make the most of your time, your energy, and your potential, it is like inheriting a great fortune: a source of abundance that transforms your life. You wake up to a new way of creativity and beauty, and you can pass your appreciation on to others.

In everyday terms, acting skillfully means doing things in a professional way by relying on your own resources. For instance, seeing skillfully means being able to judge accurately what is going on and make good decisions. Seeing with panoramic awareness means making fewer mistakes, so that the time and energy you invest in your efforts pay substantial dividends. This process of perfecting your capacities is transformative at a deep level. By contemplating your situation thoughtfully, learning to be aware of each detail, and cultivating a sense of the progression of time across days or weeks or years, you can learn to act accurately and efficiently. You can produce work of high quality, inspire those around you, and discover that challenges are what make life worthwhile. Business is a wonderful arena for working in this way because it constantly asks you to produce, and this ongoing challenge brings you alive. There are enormous benefits—both spiritual and practical. Compared to others, or compared to your own past performance, you steadily improve over time. You are gaining the knowledge you need to conduct your life in the best way.

Working 'In'

When you work with Skillful Means, you do not just work for or to; you work in—in the mind, in time, in energy, in space. You do not just learn skills, but learn who you are and how to develop your inner capacities: your knowledge, your communications, your decision-making. You discover how to use the raw materials for success and spiritual fulfillment alike: contemplation, awareness, energy, and time. Fully engaged, doing your best, you contribute to the success of the business and guarantee your own deep satisfaction. You can be loyal to your work because of what it gives you; in fact, there is no separation between you and your work. Because it does not descend upon you like an outside force, work does not produce pressure and stress; instead, it provides opportunities to taste the joy of meeting new challenges.

Working in this way, you discover that you can embody experience as you go along, drawing on each new event to develop more skill and greater knowledge. Learning through each activity, you realize that learning itself is knowledge, and prepare yourself to become a master of learning. The more you learn, the more full and meaningful life becomes. Because you are using the abundance of knowledge available to you, your actions automatically generate inspiring results. You yourself become the source of success.

I have sometimes thought that if there were just one person in the world who worked solely for the joy and challenge of working, that person could work magic. That individual would be the one true economist, the one real expert, the unparalleled investor, knowing how to hit every target. He or she would be the irrepressible magician of work, knowing how to invest in knowledge so that knowledge itself becomes the means to success. For such a person, work would have fulfilled its potential as a spiritual practice. It would hold out the promise that each of us could do anything—create anything!

Sharing the Experiment

In 1987, my student Arnaud Maitland had come to the end of his four-year term as Dean of the Nyingma Institute. Even though he had no experience with printing, he was devoted to the teachings, and especially to the practice of Skillful Means, and I asked him if he would like to work at our commercial printing operation, helping it maximize its financial contribution to our Dharma work. As a result of these discussions, Arnaud and some other students founded a company known as Dharma Enterprises. Originally he and I had thought the new business would continue in existence for only five years, but since its financial contribution to our Dharma projects proved very important, it ultimately continued to operate for ten years before being sold. Throughout this time, Arnaud worked very intensively, and he got good results. He also deepened his understanding of Skillful Means and was able to share this knowledge with others, both in formal classes and programs and more informally with his fellow workers and the members of our community.

This book grows out of the discoveries that Arnaud made while he was working at Dharma Enterprises and at the Nyingma Institute. It presents an example of how it is possible to work with Skillful Means, producing tangible benefits while simultaneously practicing a spiritual path. It is a kind of success story, just as many of our other projects have been success stories. I am proud of the work our community has done and the results they have obtained, which send ripples of positive energy through space and time.

The story Arnaud tells here could be understood as a report on an experiment. It shows that we can work without pressure or pushing ourselves, that we do not have to rely on fear, greed, and similar emotions to get good results. It shows that work is not just a means to an end, but can be intrinsically meaningful; it demonstrates that accepting challenges as they come gives richness and depth to life. Working in this way brings upaya and prajna to the West in a new form.

As readers of this book, each of you should feel free to conduct your own experiment with new ways of working. Parts of Skillful Means practice are subtle, but there are also aspects that anyone can put into effect right away. It is useful to see how someone else has been able to get results and to read about new approaches that you can implement to make success more likely. But it is more important to develop your own skillful means, based on your specific background and temperament, your own personal approach.

Skillful Means is not just a specific set of techniques. It is a way of putting knowledge to work, producing results that everyone is free to celebrate. For those of you with spiritual concerns, Skillful Means teaches that you can make your life far richer and more fulfilling. You do not have to go off to a monastery; you can practice in the present, with the job you have right now. You are free to become an entrepreneur in the marketplace of achievement and inner fulfillment, taking matters into your own hands. The knowledge you need is already available. As you march toward success, you can find enjoyment and fulfillment in whatever you do, and you can make a difference.

The work you do can be your psychology, your philosophy, and your plan for fulfillment. Work well, and you will have no regrets about what you have done with your life. I hope you learn for yourself that this is so, exercising your own capacities to the fullest. Then you can report back to the rest of us on your own journey of discovery.

Tarthang Tulku
Odiyan, USA
November 1999

Introduction:
Path to Success

Knowledge, freedom, and responsibility are our most
valuable assets, the essential ingredients for our growth and
prosperity. With them our potential for growth is unlimited.

In 1959, when the Chinese government took control
of Tibet, thousands of Tibetans went into exile. One
of them was Tarthang Tulku, a highly educated Tibetan
lama. In 1969 he established himself in the United
States. Settling in Berkeley, California, he founded the
Tibetan Nyingma Meditation Center to sustain the wisdom of the threatened Tibetan culture. Thus a pro-
phecy by Padmasambhava, who brought Buddhism to
Tibet in the eighth century, came true:

When the iron bird flies and horses run on wheels,
the Tibetan people will be scattered like ants
across the face of the world,
and the Dharma will come to the Land of the Red-faced Men.

The dramatic and cruel turn of events in Tibet brought good fortune to many of us in the West. For the first time Westerners gained access to the ancient teachings of wisdom and compassion refined for over a thousand years in Tibet, which had benefited so many people over the centuries. Tarthang Tulku arrived in the United States with the aim of preserving from extinction the vast literature and art of Tibetan Buddhism, and especially that of the Nyingma lineage to which he belongs. Moreover, he was determined to offer this culture insights and methods that would complement the Western understanding of the mind. The numerous books he has written and published, the translations he has sponsored or undertaken, and the companies he has founded—Dharma Publishing and Press, Odiyan Retreat Center, the Nyingma Institute and others—all speak of Rinpoche's care and determination, and of the depth and breadth of the teachings he represents.

Over the past thirty years, countless Western students like me have been inspired and guided by Tarthang Tulku, known to his students as Rinpoche. In 1971 I completed my studies for a degree in law in the Netherlands. For five years I worked for a large international shipping company in New York and Hong Kong. But then I made a major shift, deciding to dedicate my time and energy to working and studying under Rinpoche's guidance.

Why did I make this change? Basically because Rinpoche's teachings make perfect sense, and are so utterly positive. The philosophy and psychology of

Tibetan Buddhism is all about the awakening of human potential, drawing out what is best over time. The heart of the teachings is the recognition of our intrinsic freedom, from which we fall away over and over again, mostly out of habit and ignorance. As Rinpoche once put it, the Buddha's teachings are all about 'making things lighter'.

Warmed by recognizing the value of these truths, I began to study at the Nyingma Institute in Berkeley, California. A few years later, I received an MA in Tibetan Buddhist Philosophy and Psychology. Through studying these teachings I made a most important discovery: We already have all the knowledge we need to be successful. To awaken this knowledge and return to the authenticity of being, and to help others who wish to do the same, has become my mission in life. One sentence from the teachings in particular reflects my motivation: . . . *to lead a life that in retrospect seems worthwhile.*

Yet that was not my only motivation. In his teaching for the West, Rinpoche emphasized work as a method for spiritual growth that at the same time lets us be useful, and this spoke to me. A sentence from his book *Skillful Means* has inspired me for over twenty years: *Life exacts a price for less than full participation.*

I was particularly stimulated by participating in two large projects that achieved success against great odds. Working on these projects, we became familiar with gut energy and creativity, and managed to accomplish more than we had ever imagined possible, under exceptionally tight deadlines. I realized from this experience that a small group of enthusiastic and dedicated people could accomplish things that professionals in the field considered impossible.

This way of working, which Rinpoche called Skillful Means, was one that I wanted to make my own, and that is what I set out to do. Although it has not always been easy, there has never been a doubt in my mind that I am using my time well. I have learned a great deal about work as a training ground, as a way to develop the mind and open the heart, and a means to contribute to the betterment of this world. That is the topic of this book.

The Art of Working

Most of life is spent working, one way or another. Many people feel unhappy about this. Working for someone else or making a living without being appreciated for it may seem like a waste of time. Work may appear to be an energy drain, preventing us from doing what we really long to do, being who we really want to be. But once we realize that working is our life, we will find that in our work, more than in any other area, it is possible to be creatively and dynamically engaged. On any level, in any job, we can explore and pursue how we would like to be. At the very least, we can choose to make the activity of working into a positive effort, directed towards goals that we value and cherish.

How we work is who we are. In pursuing the art of working, we can find a way to appreciate ourselves, to foster the satisfaction of working well, and attain the enjoyment of accomplishments. We can tap into the resources that fuel personal joy and professional success in equal measure. Through the exploration of these inner resources, we can grow in personal and spiritual terms, while at the same time benefitting the organization we work for.

Learning to work well is an art that can be mastered. Once we establish a relationship with what we do and the way we work, we can learn to elevate the level at which we apply ourselves. To develop *what* we do with our time, *when* we act, and *how* we work—that is the art of working. In the process of training in this art, we become familiar with our own energy and may also learn to master the mind. We end up experts at working well, and find the source for satisfaction, enjoyment, and success.

Working with everyday obstacles, learning to deal with frustrations, and pursuing the new possibilities work offers day after day—these are both the essential ingredients of a gratifying personal life and the foundation for the growth of an organization or company. While we work, the results we get will give us immediate feedback; they mirror our attitude on the job. If we are absent-minded or dreamy, or caught up in internal dialogues, the results will tell. Mistakes will probably occur; deadlines may be missed, conflicts and misunderstandings will arise. Yet deep down we know it is possible to take full responsibility. In taking responsibility we take hold of our lives and get a grip on the success of any endeavor. The secret of this success is to work hard and to have faith in getting results.

A Classic Business Story with a Twist

For ten challenging and inspiring years, a small core group applied Skillful Means at Dharma Enterprises, a commercial press that grew out of the operations of Dharma Press, one of the non-profit companies that Rinpoche founded to accomplish his aims. Founded in 1987, and intended from the outset as a business venture with a limited life span, Dharma Enterprises offered my co-workers and me the opportunity to study the principles of Skillful Means from many different angles.

It was a journey of adventure, at once a business opportunity and a chance to practice Tibetan Buddhism in daily life. We could earn a livelihood for ourselves and generate income that would provide a livelihood for many others, while also making substantial contributions to the preservation of ancient texts and art. Again and again experts told us we were being too ambitious; that we were setting impossible goals. Yet we had a vision. We had the motivation. We had faith based on experience. We set out to give form to what we knew to be true—that time, money, and spiritual development work together well.

The team that started Dharma Enterprises consisted largely of novices, with little general business experience and still less specific knowledge of the printing industry. As we went along we acquired many new skills. We learned how to run a business, and more specifically we got acquainted with the craft of printing. We learned how to motivate ourselves, to cooperate, to recharge our vitality while working, and most of all to get results. We noticed and appreciated that the results we get inform us of how we work and who we are, at the same time presenting us with the tools for change. Gradually our vision took on a much more specific shape. In our own way we began to embody basic teachings on taking responsibility and applying gut energy to achieve our goals. The fruits were immediately apparent. In the first three years of operations, the company quadrupled its sales to six million dollars a year. And throughout its existence it continued to enjoy healthy profits. Ours is a classic success story, but with a twist.

Mastering Work

This book began as a modest project to document the history of a company, Dharma Enterprises: a chronicle of what we had done with ten years of our lives. When I mentioned the idea to Rinpoche, he not only approved of it, but added: "Why don't you write a book on how to run a successful company?" This came as a surprise, although in the introduction to his book *Mastering Successful Work*, Rinpoche encourages everyone to write his or her own book on how to use time well. And so I set to work.

Certainly *MasterWork* has been written in the spirit of sharing what all of us at Dharma Enterprises learned during our ten-year quest. Rinpoche's visionary force is behind every page, and his teaching, as expressed in three books—*Skillful Means, Mastering Successful Work,* and *Knowledge of Freedom*—informs its content. Rinpoche himself has developed Skillful Means into an inspiring and powerful management training system. We had the opportunity to put this system into practice. My hope is that this record of our discoveries will encourage others to investigate these methods and verify their value for themselves, both on an individual level and the success for the company.

MasterWork is divided into two parts. Part One (Chapters 1–3) introduces Dharma Enterprises, in many ways a regular commercial printing company battling with everyday problems: how to get clients and how to keep them; how to establish quality and how to maintain it; how to stay ahead of the competition; how to deliver the product on time; and last but not least, how to pay the bills in spite of continuing cash flow problems. What distinguished us from other printing companies was our commitment to the Skillful Means Management Training. Dharma Enterprises is a manifestation of what we did with Rinpoche's vision of how to run a profitable business, of how we turned theory into practice. Rinpoche attributed the success of Dharma Enterprises to our practice of Skillful Means at work.

Part Two presents some of the Skillful Means topics that helped us develop a creative and positive attitude towards time, meet high standards of quality, increase productivity, benefit the bottom line, inspire the employees, and foster a solid team spirit. Like the chapters in Part One these seven chapters contain a host of examples, as well as practices drawn initially from Tarthang Tulku's teachings that we put into effect in daily application, *while* working. The themes of the chapters in Part Two are as follows:

4 **Wisdom in Action:** Daily activities to attain and express the highest wisdom

5 **Mastering Time:** Making time central in our lives, and drawing on its dynamic vitality and knowledge to realize our goals

6 **Instant Success:** Promoting leadership through wholehearted participation to improve communication, cooperation, and responsibility

7 **Positive Knowledge:** Learning to guard against negativity and strengthen what is positive for growth

8 **Inner Resources:** The resources to be successful—awareness, concentration, and energy

9 **Questioning Mind:** Discovering that we already have the knowledge we need to be successful

10 **Meditation, Just Being:** Learning to meditate while we work, to become calm and clear and expand our mind in time and space

11 **Quality on Time:** The importance of productivity, efficiency, and profit to both the individual and the company

If you take the themes and exercises in these chapters to heart and practice them, you will find that the situation at work and the results you get soon improve.

Working with Skillful Means every day for ten years, we learned to consider work as a path of knowledge, a spiritual journey. Anyone can create within himself the opportunity for a similar undertaking or enterprise.

MasterWork

Skillful Means provides maps to the unknown territories we enter on this journey. They may guide us at many different levels, depending on our predisposition and personal situation. But one thing is certain. No matter where we start or how we proceed, we will soon begin to appreciate and take advantage of the opportunities that work provides.

Work will teach us how to develop the mind, create a positive atmosphere, improve our level of energy, and overcome obstacles. The methods of Skillful Means encourage us to care about what we do with our lives and what we accomplish, while dedicating the results to a greater cause. Our own well-being and that of others, the success of the organization we work for, and even the health of the society at large will gradually improve. Working in this way, we participate in a timeless, never-ending story, as time perpetually offers fresh possibilities for growth and ample opportunities for a satisfying life.

MasterWork

PART ONE

Vision–Path–Goals

1

Meeting Financial Commitments

*Our success or failure—and the success or failure
of the company or organization for which we work—
ultimately depends on our willingness
as individuals to be responsible.*

On a warm summer day in 1987, a meeting was held
on the lawn of Padma Ling, the building that
houses the head office of the Nyingma organizations,
in Berkeley, California. It was attended by the board
members of Dharma Press operations and chaired
by Tarthang Tulku, an accomplished Tibetan lama in
exile, the founder of Dharma Press and all the Nyingma
organizations.

In 1959, Tarthang Tulku (known to his students as
Rinpoche) was on retreat in the mountain kingdom of
Bhutan, having left Tibet a year earlier to continue his
studies with his own teacher. In March of that year, the
Chinese government seized control of Tibet, and

5

Rinpoche realized he could not return to his native land. He soon settled in Varanasi, India, and in 1962 he started a printing and publishing company to produce and distribute Buddhist texts in Tibetan that were now threatened with extinction. After moving to the United States in the late sixties, he reestablished these operations under the names Dharma Publishing and Dharma Press. The purpose of these companies was to preserve ancient Tibetan Buddhist texts and to introduce their teachings in the West. They have since become the leading Buddhist publishing operation in the West. In the late seventies Dharma Press engaged in commercial printing as part of its training program, and in 1985, as the commercial operations expanded, a new company was created to develop this commercial potential in ways consistent with Buddhist teachings. Now we were about to transfer these operations to a newly formed company, and I would be its president.

We were gathered to discuss the plans for this new venture, starting later that year. As the representative of this future enterprise, I asked Rinpoche how he envisioned success for the new company. Without a moment's hesitation, he answered: "Make it a first-class business, meet your financial commitments, and bring the Dharma there."

The meeting focused on the financial commitments and how to start up the activities. By the end of the day, it had been agreed that the Nyingma organizations would lend the new company money to buy the equipment for a bindery, and later for printing presses. But that was not all. The newborn child would inherit an ongoing business with an excellent client list, would have access to training in all aspects of running a commercial press, and last but not least, would have the right to use the name Dharma Enterprises. Receiving this name was pivotal, as it implied that we would have access to the Dharma teachings for daily application, under Rinpoche's guidance. And in fact, this proved to be the case. Over the next ten years we received extensive materials on Skillful Means, through manuals, papers, oral instructions, and suggestions for meditations and visualizations. Skillful Means presented the Dharma in daily life. Thus, Dharma Enterprises became an authentic Dharma center.

As a symbol of this link, Dharma Enterprises received a logo designed by Rinpoche, consisting of a moon on a lotus flower. As with other Dharma symbols, this logo had a power and significance that went beyond conceptual thinking and explanations. For me personally, the value of this logo for our company was comparable to the importance of the moon to the earth.

The connection with Dharma allowed Dharma Enterprises to attract the kind of employees it was looking for. Whoever applied for a job knew they might receive lower wages than the industry average. But they also knew that by offering Dharma Enterprises their services they could learn and be useful at the same time. They would have the chance to develop their inner resources, in accord with Buddhist teachings, as well as the satisfaction of contributing to Dharma projects. Inspired by this vision and the challenge of the venture, all of us, as founding members and employees of

Dharma Enterprises, were content with minimal monetary compensation. Personally, I have always felt I received more than I gave. We knew that by learning the secret of effective and rewarding work, we would be spending our time well.

The license agreement between Dharma Enterprises and the parent company of Dharma Press governed many of these points, and it also set financial commitments. As of March 1988, Dharma Enterprises would pay royalties in the amount of $45,000 per month, gradually increasing over eighteen months to $75,000 per month.

Since the lifeline to the Dharma and the opportunity to provide financial benefits for the Dharma were pivotal to the entire set-up, we agreed that paying the royalties would be our top priority. They would be paid, not as an afterthought or in case the funds were available, but *before* anything else. In other words: the royalties would have precedence over all other expenses, including taxes, payroll, overhead and supplies. That afternoon, as the sun began to set while we were sitting in a lovely garden framed by a background of interwoven bamboo trees, someone turned to me and asked, with disbelief in her voice: "Do you realize what you are committing yourselves to?"

Royalties

Setting the monthly royalty payments at a fixed amount was important to both parties involved. From Dharma Press' perspective the benefit was obvious; a fixed revenue would enable them to budget with confidence for the major projects they had in the works. As for Dharma Enterprises, a monthly payment would be an opportunity and a challenge to maximize our inner resources. Making a fixed financial commitment reached deep into us. Here, beyond likes and dislikes, fear and worries, the founding members and employees of the company would find each other. A more usual royalty, based on a percentage of sales, would not have been half as stimulating; in effect it would have rewarded poor performance. And there was another benefit. Whatever we made in excess of the royalties was pure profit.

Over the years, several informed observers have challenged us about the royalties: Did we not feel they were inordinately high (at that time about sixteen percent of sales)? Many people thought this was an impossible burden. In the early 1990s, I visited an accountant in San Francisco—a professor in tax law at a local university—to review our financial situation. After studying the data, he looked up at me and said, "I'm glad I'm not in your shoes.'

Without being flippant, I can say that I was glad not to be in his shoes either. When he said, "What you are trying to do is impossible," he plainly exhibited the limits of his world. In his mind, the royalties we had committed to pay meant that we were always on the edge of survival, if not in fact already bankrupt. Yet another way of looking at it was that if the payments were burdensome, this meant that our sales were simply not high enough. Had our sales continued to increase at the rate they did during the first three years, after about five years the royalties would have amounted to six percent of sales. Nobody would have criticized or questioned that amount.

The truth is that for ten years we were a healthy, ongoing business. We were debt-free and always paid our bills. On average, we provided forty people or more with their daily livelihood for over a decade. And after paying full royalties, our profits were still above average in the industry. If we had paid more typical royalties—say, five percent of sales—the profits we generated as a percentage of sales would have far exceeded those of even the industry leaders. How to explain that? Without the licensing agreement, we would not have been able to start up at all, nor could we have survived. The agreement actually proved to be an excellent deal for both parties.

It is true that we were helped by the fact that a small percentage of our total workforce (varying between thirty-five and seventy-five people over the years), the workers who practiced Skillful Means, received wages that were below market value. Still, those savings were more than offset by the expenses we incurred in doing printing at no charge for Dharma Publishing, as our direct contribution to its Dharma work.

Although in the early years our financial situation was precarious, we invariably managed to meet our commitments, month after month. Generally speaking, this made everything easier. It seems that money needs to flow. Holding back, based on fear, only inhibits the general stream of energy and of well-being, including that of money and work, and as a result possibilities dry up. By making payments, even partial ones, the flow becomes steady and stable. I experienced each monthly payment to the Dharma as being like a blessing, generating new print orders. This became very evident when in the last year of Dharma Enterprises' operation, royalty payments were reduced substantially, and it suddenly proved more difficult to make the lower payments in full and on time.

Paying the Bills

Right from the beginning, paying the bills on time was our guiding principle. Frankly, we did not have much choice, for Dharma Enterprises was run one month at a time. After a print order had come in, we would purchase the necessary materials. In fact, everything was purchased on an 'as needed' basis. Usually the bills had to be paid by the tenth of the following month. But in our operation, with the production time required, our clients might not pay their invoices to us until the beginning of the third month after an order came in. This gap in the cash flow created great financial pressure. On the first of every month we had to make the royalty payment, in addition to paying the suppliers; at the end of the month, when the payroll and (quarterly) sales tax came due, the pressure would rise to a boiling point.

The way we dealt with this was by arranging for an extension of the payment terms by the supplier to the last day of the second month. We were able to do this and still take a two percent discount for paying on time. We also tried to persuade our clients to pay up front for their work, or at least make payments early.

Our strategy with bills was to pay the big paper companies first, as they gave a discount for prompt payment, and as they were capable of turning off the tap instantly. Early on, we decided to meet with the presidents of our three major paper suppliers. They were invited to our facilities to show them that the presses were running constantly and to meet the people who made up our company. We took them out to lunch and convinced them that we were a good credit risk. Too much was at stake, too many organizations and individuals depending on us, for us ever to go bankrupt. On their initiative, payment schedules were arranged that were extremely favorable to us. In less than five months, we were paying within the discount period, saving two percent on each paper purchase—$25,000 per year. From then on we were more aggressive in our paper purchasing, always intent on getting the sharpest price. Still, we remained loyal to our original suppliers, especially to those who had been the most generous in the payment schedules.

The smallest suppliers, such as the stationery suppliers and knife sharpeners for the cutter, were next on our priority list. Often they were family-run business operators who could not afford to wait for their money, and we wanted to accommodate them. Furthermore, we could not be bothered with endless phone calls for relatively minor amounts of money.

The middle group of suppliers, such as the ink companies, were at the bottom of the list. To make up for this, we gave them maximum personal attention. It took us a few years to begin paying them on time, and to receive their discounts for paying within schedule.

Relations with the bank were tense at first, but gradually grew increasingly friendly. On many days, the manager of the local bank branch would call to inform us we had an overdraft. Personal visits to our premises convinced him each time that lots of activity was going on, and that we would eventually meet our obligations.

Once we tried to bridge the gap between incoming and outgoing cash by arranging for a line of credit with the bank. Instead of meeting with our branch manager, however, we received a visit from a young woman we had never met before. In our modest conference room, she took one look at the financial statement, which reflected our continuous negative cash flow, and said, "I am very sorry, but we cannot help you." We had no choice but to continue to juggle our finances creatively for the next few years.

We had enough reasons to be nervous, and at times I lay awake at night, worrying about the cash flow and the need for more sales. Still, deep down I never lost faith. I was positive we would make it, even if all the odds seemed to be against us. Sometimes I felt that our commitment to a good cause reflected back to us the support we so desperately needed. There is an ancient saying in the Dharma teachings: "If you bow down to the Dharma, it reflects back a thousandfold."

Setting Goals

Keeping financial commitments taught us that if we are dedicated to a goal, how we actually get there will more or less unfold by itself. The difficulties and obstacles we encountered often indicated that the target was not clearly laid out, or that we had ignored the guiding vision. Once we made up our mind, the vision seemed to inform us of what to do next, bringing the goal to life once more.

In any business or work, there is always a vision beckoning to us in the distance. Once we recognize the signs, our longing to achieve the vision will draw us forward, even if it remains uncertain where it will lead us next, or how and when we will reach the goal. We find ourselves on the journey of a lifetime, with the goal like a compass in the back of our minds. If we hold it there and keep a light focus on it, it will certainly show us the way, sooner or later.

Once the overarching vision is in place, the plans and priorities figuring foremost in our minds may change from day to day. We can direct our attention to three or four things simultaneously, as long as they sprout from the vision at the back of the mind. We can let ourselves be the instrument of our vision. The more clear and encompassing the image, the more stable and expansive the results of our actions will be. At Dharma Enterprises, the practice of Skillful Means helped us to articulate and strengthen the goal in the back of our minds, while individual responsibility

14

stayed foremost in our minds. In daily activity these two blended into the practice of caring.

At that first meeting, Rinpoche had told us to meet our financial commitments, run a first-class business, and bring the Dharma into our operations. In practice, we found that these three principles strongly supported each other. Foremost in our minds was to serve the clients and execute the jobs fast and well; in other words, to run a first-class business. In the back of our minds we held the 'all-inclusive' guideline: "Pay the bills on time." The merging of these principles was our way to bring the Dharma there. The components of these three guidelines were actually interchangeable. We could focus on any of these, and all three would come into view. Together, they provided the vision for our efforts, defined the path of action, and yielded results.

Action

Making our financial commitments under our license agreement with Dharma Press our top priority demanded creativity, dedication, effort, and follow-through. Skillful Means taught us that these qualities help both the individual and the corporation to grow, and for us this proved to be true. On top of that, we never forgot that the money we paid was destined for Dharma projects. This was a potent symbol for our fundamental aim: to work successfully while also practicing the Dharma.

Dharma is a term for the Buddhist teachings. Dharma practice is essentially a path of self-knowledge.

For those who engage with it wholeheartedly, Dharma is not just worship, prayer or meditation, but daily application on how to make oneself and others healthy, happy, and successful.

As a guideline for action, Dharma implies doing what is right or appropriate to the situation. In the context of business, this means that the success and integrity of the company depend on the attitudes and actions of the workers. In order for the results of action to be Dharma, they must be positive for everyone involved—the workers, stockholders or members, clients, and suppliers, and beyond that for all sentient beings.

Those who work successfully, or are determined to do so, are already on the way towards a Dharma practice. Dharma is more than a particular set of teachings. To consider work as a training ground or a means to wake up to knowledge, and to hold respect for the well-being of others as the overarching principle, is to act in accord with the Dharma. Other qualities required for Dharma practice, such as responsibility, commitment, and follow-through, are equally indispensable to succeed in business. The joy of such an approach, central in Skillful Means, is in the uniting of two seemingly separate aims: the growth of the individual and the benefit of others.

Benefits

Looking back, it is clear that meeting the financial commitments was one of the most rewarding aspects of our work at Dharma Enterprises. Our royalty payments, in excess of eight million dollars over ten years, contributed to a great variety of causes: the publication of a massive collection of Tibetan texts known as Great Treasures of Nyingma Teachings, stipends for Nyingma community members, the production of prayer wheels, building and reforestation at the Odiyan Retreat Center, and various other Dharma projects. A portion of the royalties also went toward the support of monasteries in India, Nepal, Tibet, and Bhutan. One day, as Rinpoche was leaving the premises after one of his visits, he said to us, "Thank you very much. You are our bread and butter."

Setting goals, getting results, appreciating the benefits—their interplay was the key to the success of Dharma Enterprises. In time we found they were also the essence of the practice of Skillful Means. You start with an idea, a vision. While working to realize this vision, you learn from the results, and also from your mistakes. Your skills improve, and you become more successful in both our professional and personal lives. In a way, it is all very simple.

2

A First-Class Business

*If we use work to challenge our limits,
to perfect awareness and deepen concentration,
then work can open into knowledge that makes us
more successful while also nourishing us at the deepest level.*

At the time Dharma Enterprises was founded, there were 450 commercial printers in the San Francisco Bay Area. If Dharma Enterprises were to successfully position itself in that arena, it would indeed have to become a first-class business—and fast. Since Skillful Means emphasizes the power of deadlines, it seemed appropriate that meeting our clients' deadlines should become the basis for our niche in the market. Therefore, we focused on excellent service and on prompt delivery. Our slogans were 'Dharma Enterprises offers you the best' and 'You can relax with Dharma'. The trucks that made deliveries carried the motto 'Quality on Time', referring not only to the product, but also to our interactions and to the integrity of the company.

In running our business we always took the point of view and the potential advantages of all parties into consideration. What would be good for the members of Dharma Enterprises (our equivalent of stockholders)? What would benefit the employees, the clients, the suppliers, our affiliated organizations, and even the environment at large? A first-class deal is one from which each party concerned benefits. Putting that notion into practice required a first-class mind-set and a first-class attitude. Little by little, the vision began to take shape. In our minds, becoming a first-class business boiled down to three things: Getting results, making good business decisions, and last but not least, enjoying the experience

Getting Results

From the first day, it seemed that the best we had to offer was to start into action immediately. There was no need for elaborate plans or extensive meetings, and we were confident we would learn the trade as we went along. What mattered was to get results quickly. The bills had to be paid, and therefore we needed more print orders, less spoilage, faster turnaround. As we set into motion, we regularly reminded each other of the original guidelines. Often the question was put directly: What would a first-class business do in this case? Invariably the answer was that it would excel in time as well as in quality. Our selling point became speed. We were willing to work six days a week in order to meet the client's demands, and since we were accustomed to working fast, giving good service was not really an extra effort. It was providing quality that required our special attention.

Saturdays were special for us. Often we were a skeleton crew. Undisturbed by phones and faxes, we could energetically whip up a high level of production. It was usually a most satisfying day, topped off by a short Skillful Means class and a closing ceremony on the roof of the building.

Customers were delighted we could meet their deadlines, but often we were even more motivated than the customer to get the job done. We were naturally driven by the pressures of financial commitments—to get the discounts for prompt payments and pay off debts. We also simply enjoyed working fast. Being inexperienced, we sometimes lost track of details or fell short on quality. But we learned our lesson the hard way: Mistakes led either to reprinting the job or to losing the customer. We were forced to modify our hurry-up attitudes, setting a rule: If it comes to a choice between time and quality, always opt for quality!

In our enthusiasm for high energy and full speed, lapses in communication could occur. There was a tendency to make assumptions, and jump to conclusions. To restore the ensuing damage, quick, one-minute meetings were often necessary. Down in the pressroom, a few words would be enough. It was stimulating to see this essential communication take shape.

Due to the focus on speed, some employees saw our operation as chaotic in comparison to other work places. Yet others flourished on this way of working at full steam, and most of us felt the 'all-at-once-approach', as we called it, stimulated dynamic creativity, stirring up seething energy. Those who preferred the linear approach, thinking about one job at a time, eventually either left or turned around and joined the team more wholeheartedly.

Gut Energy

During the first years we did not need many motivational meetings; Dharma Enterprises was our baby, and we wanted it to grow up strong. Its health and survival depended on our motivation and gut energy to get things done. Time was the single most motivational factor. There was simply not enough time for doubt or inner dialogues. Cooperation became natural. Skillful Means taught us that everybody is his own boss; that the pressman, for example, should consider his press as a small enterprise, with its specific materials, maintenance, and potential to produce.

In order to work productively at a gut level, there has to be a balance. Planning is essential. The client's needs, the workflow, and our capabilities blended together, keeping us on our toes. But planning and gut energy both relate to time: When will the job come in; when will the proof be ready; when will the client do a job-check on the press; how long will it take to print the job; when does it go to the bindery operators; what day can we guarantee delivery? We were constantly pushed by time. Together with the clients' demands, time was our life and our guide.

21

During those first years there was hardly any time for fear or difficulties to linger. Dharma Enterprises was not the place to dwell on emotions; we simply could not afford them. We were constantly training ourselves to use our time well, and to be satisfied with our accomplishments. Instead of paying attention to the stories in our heads, we connected our work to the demands of time. Working wholeheartedly melts emotionality that would otherwise, sooner or later, show up as obstacles or mistakes. This focus began to bring about a subtle transformation. Emotional stuckness or repetition turned into positive energy.

This is not to say that we were without fear. A touch of fear or awareness of potential danger spices up the motivation and stimulates transformation. Fear of making a mistake, missing a deadline, or losing a client grabs your attention and keeps you on course. But what really mattered was the work. Printing is a blend of technical skill, quality control, and gut energy, and we had to work on all of them at the same time. Time and the rhythms of the machines activated our motivation. All that mattered was how many sheets of good quality work we could finish in the quickest time. All our inner resources were on full alert. We sensed that if these were well-tuned, satisfaction and profit would invariably be our feedback.

Working like this made us 'selfish' in an interesting way. On the one hand we could not be selfish at the expense of ignoring others or the overall good of the company; on the other hand we had to be really selfish. We told ourselves, "This job, this company is my baby

. . . my press needs to produce . . . I must get results."
Responsibility, cooperation, and a tinge of pride became a healthy mix.

First-Class Attitude

To foster a first-class attitude, we need to constantly
encourage and inspire ourselves. Then the mind spirals toward greater and greater cycles of exciting mind,
ambitious mind, enthusiastic mind, determined mind,
honest mind, smart mind, direct mind, and eager
mind. We learn to embrace opportunities as they arise.
The resulting mentality is keen and analytical, values
stability, and keeps an eye out for what is unique.

To stimulate this first-class potential, we learned to
question ourselves. How can we improve productivity
and overall organization? Are we genuinely committed
to strengthening our skills or are we just coasting
along? Such questioning generated awareness of the
way we worked. It made us more responsible and reliable, both individually and as a company. The result
was that our customers, including major corporations
such as Pacific Bell and Wells Fargo Bank, remained
loyal to us, year after year.

To develop a first-class attitude it helps to have
examples. Good role models and friends can teach us
how dedication and energy are a perfect couple. Yet an
excess of examples may be confusing. Once somebody
suggested we should read biographies of successful
people and businesses. We followed the advice and
studied 'how to' books and tapes. Although such study

unmistakably had a stimulating effect, there were simply too many ideas, too many options. The force of habit is strong, and we could not change everything at once. In fact, we sometimes had a hard time maintaining even one single change.

Starting out with a specific topic, we had to introduce it into our awareness, and then remind and inspire ourselves over and over to prevent relapses in the old ways, and to enable the fresh approach to settle as regular practice. Then, when the new habit had become routine, it would gradually lose its power. Making improvements felt like an ongoing battle against old patterns and opinions and the tendency to settle for less.

Spending much of our time on fixing problems, we certainly became first-class in finding solutions. However, the intense involvement in making everyday things work made us lose track of the general goal of becoming a first-class business. Frenetic activity may mask feelings of complacency and lack of ambition. The constant busyness made us tolerant towards our fears, and unwilling to question weaknesses. Whenever we accepted the pressure of work at face value, our attitude began to slump. Again and again we had to start afresh, going back to core values and concerns, restating our goals and committing to them. We let ourselves be guided by the question, "What is really important?" We came back to focusing on the benefits of work, and most importantly, on getting results. Challenging our ways of working at this more basic level was a way to spark improvement. When we could do it, it invariably bred success.

First-Class Equipment

First-class equipment is indispensable for getting good results on a lasting basis. Anyway, enjoying the experience of working is not easy when the equipment keeps breaking down. Our bindery equipment was new and of good quality, but the printing equipment was a different story. To accommodate the expanding sales, we put back into service a fifty-year-old 65-inch two-color press, as well as a one-color press that had sat idle for a number of years. All the presses were running twenty-four hours a day, six days a week.

Eventually this situation became unworkable. Our clients had to wait for ten days or more to get on press, and business was still growing. It was clear we had to buy another press.

As we researched the options, everyone advised us to choose another two-color press, since that was the technology we already knew. Instead, we decided on a far more expensive four-color press. A four-color press —using the primary colors of yellow, magenta, and cyan, plus black—can print any color composition, providing a finished product all at once, and our clients had ample four-color process work to give us. We were influenced by the fact that in Tibetan Buddhism different colors are said to stimulate different qualities and abilities of both body and mind. We were also eager to learn new skills, and looked forward to working with full color.

It all happened very fast. There was a visit to the Heidelberg showroom, the most renowned manufacturer of printing presses. Without hesitation we settled on a new four-color 40-inch press, perfect for our market. The sticker price of $1.3 million was steep, but it did not scare us away. We made an offer of $960,000. The sales manager insisted they could go no lower than $982,000. Although it was tempting to give in, we held to our offer. As it turned out, the end of a business quarter was approaching, and the sales staff had to make a quota based on units sold. The deal went through.

The new press was scheduled for delivery in November, 1989. In October there was a major earthquake in the San Francisco Bay area, with serious damage right outside our door. Momentarily everything came to a complete stop. It was most shocking to see a collapsed double-decker freeway up close. For a short time we let go of our focus on speed and quality, on clients and money, and a deep caring for people and safety became all-absorbing. The earthquake would have an impact on people and business for years to come. For example, one of our clients in San Francisco decided not to do business with companies across the Bay such as ours for fear they would be inaccessible during a catastrophe.

A few weeks after the earthquake, three huge flat-bed trucks pulled up at seven o'clock in the morning. Each one carried a piece of the new press covered with orange cloth, like statues waiting to be unveiled. It took four weeks to set it up, but by the end of December it was plain to see: With this piece of equipment in place, we were a first-class business at every level.

Having the new press in the shop felt like having a dinosaur over for dinner. It was always hungry, ready for more jobs. It printed seven times as fast as the old 65-inch press, and about three times as fast as our two-color press. We hired an expert to guide us through the first years, while we sharpened our own skills. In the meantime, however, productivity had sunk below acceptable norms. To make up for the shortfall, we asked a Dharma worker to step in and become the lead pressman on the new press. Usually the lead pressman on a comparable press serves an apprenticeship of several years, but working with Skillful Means methods makes it possible to learn new skills relatively quickly. In no time at all he was turning out excellent work, and our productivity increased dramatically. From then on the new Heidelberg press carried the major load.

Technical Changes

In the early 1990s a major technological change swept through the printing business. Design and layout had up to that time been done by hand on art boards which were presented to the printer to make film. Now this work was increasingly being done with computers, and very soon the jobs were delivered on disk. Most printing companies tend to stick to what they know best and what pays well, sending out other parts of the job. However, we chose to keep most steps of manufacturing to ourselves. Since we did not want to depend on outside contractors to do the film work that arrived on disk, we decided to purchase the new electronic prepress equipment that would allow us to handle computer-generated text and art. That way, we could control quality and, even more important, scheduling. Total costs for the new equipment came to $400,000, which we paid off within two years. Now we had state-of-the-art equipment in every department. All that was necessary to stay a first-class business.

Good Business Decisions

For any business, making good decisions implies aiming for lasting positive solutions, thinking in the short term and the long term simultaneously, having an eye for both detail and overview, and drawing out the best in people. All parties must benefit from any deal. This was a real challenge for Dharma Enterprises, whose strength lay in action rather than reflection. We were used to getting results by relying on stamina, creativity, and good intentions. Planning and thinking through consequences was a different matter.

First-Class Mind

Like any good teacher, Rinpoche regularly brought attention to what was out of balance. Often he would tell us, "You need more heads." Initially, we thought this meant we should hire outside experts, and sometimes we did, but we came to see it more as an encouragement to exercise our own intelligence.

A first-class mind is not just about intelligence. Such a mind is smart and imaginative, and has ambition, enthusiasm, honesty, and discipline. And most of all it is gutsy. At ease with the overarching vision and loyal to it, the first-class business mind is geared toward profit and success. Like an athlete who exercises and challenges his talents to excel and to win, the creative business person challenges his capabilities, rising above the ordinary toward the highest quality, performance, and innovation.

Seen in this light, Dharma Enterprises had the flavor of a business school. The company offered training for people who intended to develop a first-class mind, a practical education in refining human qualities and resources. But bringing this idea to life was far from easy. For one thing, recruiting the right people was difficult. Job applicants who were mainly concerned about controlling their own time and about remuneration would not be likely to benefit from working at Dharma Enterprises. On the other hand, if someone seemed eager to accept simply any assignment, we knew from experience that this intention might soon change. Only on the job do people show their true colors.

In an interview our first question was always, "What would you like to learn?" The next was, "Do you like to work?" The responses we got let us sense if there was a possible match. Even after the person had been hired, these two topics remained a key point of reference.

At the start, we meant to employ only workers who were genuinely interested in studying and practicing the Skillful Means Management Training. However, the company grew faster than expected, and from the beginning we were badly in need of expertise. Therefore, the original plan of making Skillful Means the common denominator in the workforce had to be abandoned. In fact, we took care not to emphasize our commitment to Skillful Means, for fear of being accused of proselytizing.

This reticence was probably misguided. Had we been more open and outspoken about our vision of work as a tool for personal growth, we might have attracted more people who were looking for exactly this kind of challenge. The way it turned out, most of our employees were never aware of the specifics of our vision and goals and the methods we used to achieve them. This made it much harder for the core group to implement them.

A Tight Muscle

During its first years, Dharma Enterprises was primarily sales-oriented. Our cycle was built on high energy: Get the job, do it quickly, open up the press for more work, add extra people when needed. We worked overtime, and in less than four years annual sales hit their all-time peak of $6.7 million per year. At that time we had seventy-five employees, and we were constantly busy. But suddenly everything changed. First came the Loma Prieta earthquake in 1989, then a devastating fire in the East Bay, followed by the Persian Gulf War in 1991. On top of that, following a national trend, the California economy entered a prolonged slump that lasted for the next five years.

During the recession, clients put jobs on hold or canceled them altogether. Many companies decided to downsize and to simplify their printing requirements for economy reasons. For example, in 1988 we printed brochures for Wells Fargo Bank and their employee benefit programs in seven colors. A few years later, the same job was mostly one-color.

One day someone brought in a news article about Xerox instructing its divisions to reduce costs by five percent across the board. We decided to follow suit. It became exciting to tackle this project, and within one year overall expenses were reduced by thirteen percent. During this time Rinpoche encouraged us repeatedly, saying, "Become a tight muscle." We decided to reduce the workforce, even though laying off people was painful. It was noteworthy that those who were let go were in the least expensive and the most expensive segments of our workforce; for whatever reason, they seemed to be the least dynamic workers. After the changes we were down to thirty-five people. As the lines of communication grew shorter, the atmosphere and results improved dramatically.

As time went on, our focus on sales evaporated. We had a minimal sales force, and it somehow lacked the essential spirit that Dharma Enterprises was unbeatable. To deal with this, we began questioning our motivation and effort, and reminding ourselves of the type of work we could do well and fast. Something sparked, and we came out of our inertia and reconnected with the idea of exploring the market. It was striking to note how close complacency and positive energy are to one another, for it really did not require much to shift from one mood to the other. And once we had reconnected with our goals, change did not take long. The sales effort became more organized. We started to keep track of calls, visits, quotes, and jobs secured. Merely recording the facts had an uplifting impact on the entire organization. Results improved instantly, and we had soon won back our first-class attitude.

An important part of making good business decisions is picking the right clients. We had difficulties adhering to this principle. Many times we were happy to get just any client. We were committed to treating the client as king, but when the client turned out not to be right for us, this could put quite a strain on our operations. And at times clients would take advantage of their high-ranking position. Then we had a dilemma: Should we make a sacrifice and give in to the client's demands, or let the customer go and leave us emptyhanded?

The advantage was that having difficult clients kept us on our toes. We simply could not give them cause for complaints. We would go out of our way to offer the best. For instance, to assure good communication, we made it a point to confirm essential communications in writing, and to be available at all times, day or night. We were determined to fulfill our promise to deliver high quality on time, even when the cost was great. Being a servant to such a principle is both humbling and stimulating. It mobilized all our resources.

Learning how to straighten out problems with clients is a long road. When the client had a complaint and we knew we were not at fault, it was not easy to compromise. But at times we had to swallow our pride, bounce back, and be ready to be of service for the next job. Over and over, we had to refresh our commitment to a first-class attitude, and to making first-class decisions all along the way.

Of course, anyone in business is making decisions all day long. We made good decisions and bad ones, or no decisions at all. Everyone who works knows how easy it is to fall into the trap of being reactive, just extinguishing fires. Mostly this is due to poor planning or lack of anticipation, for it requires real discipline to take the time to review all the decisions of the day. But anyone can learn how to make good decisions. Awareness of the small good day-to-day decisions stimulates a positive momentum towards stability and growth.

We let this opportunity slip through our fingers, as usually only our big mistakes woke us up. We certainly had our share of bad decisions. For instance, when we got our electronic prepress equipment, we were one of the very first printers in the San Francisco Bay area to have these capabilities in-house. This strength should have been our focus. Instead, we were slow to take advantage, at once complacent and afraid to approach new customers and find the appropriate jobs. We missed opportunities to capitalize on our investment. It was like having a wonderful horse in the stable and never taking it out for a ride.

Another example came about when Pacific Bell Directory, our major customer, put out to bid all their small printing requirements, such as stationery and business cards, a contract totalling about $150,000 per year. Our good connections with that company made it seem worthwhile to try and secure this steady business. We decided to start a separate division called Dharma Express to handle this short-run, quick turnaround market. But in order to qualify, we needed to acquire small press and finishing equipment.

We hired an outside expert, created a special area on the shop floor, and bought the minimum amount of equipment required, thinking that if we got the job we would buy more machines and hire people. Then suddenly our expert disappeared from the scene. Without a qualified person to supervise our operation in the initial phases, we canceled our plans and cut our losses. In time, we realized the whole plan had been a mistake. This kind of operation, with its inherent diversification, was very labor intensive, while our aim was to achieve greater output with fewer people. In retrospect, we were fortunate that external circumstances prevented us from going in the wrong direction.

A few years later we got another chance at a Pacific Bell Directory job. A large project was available that involved mostly handwork, with almost no printing in the early phases. We had become efficient in this line of work—collating materials and packaging complex orders—as an adjunct to large print orders. We were confident we could organize and execute the job, which meant about $450,000 a year in sales. The money was appealing.

Again we set up a space, and this time we began work. It did not take long to realize that the job was substantially more complicated than we had been led to believe. For three weeks we worked at it, but the work was tedious, and it became clear that we would have to hire new employees if we wanted to do it. By then time was too short to make such a dramatic change. We knew that another company was ready to take on the job, and we decided to return the assignment to the customer. It seemed an easy decision at the time, but it was probably not the right one. We could have tried right from the outset to find new people who enjoy this kind of detailed work. It would have meant a steady source of income for years to come.

Probably the most difficult decisions were those where personnel was concerned. We often hesitated to make the necessary changes when a certain employee was not right for the job. We let people stay because we could not face the idea of going through the headache of finding a replacement. If we did decide to let someone go, we would try to have him take the initiative to leave. But some stayed on for too long, gradually undermining the spirit and reliability of the company. Opting for the status quo caused real damage, whereas if we had not been afraid to part ways, the newly created opening would have made it possible for the right person to come in, benefiting the whole organization.

Enjoying the Experience

Running a first-class business means more than getting results and making good decisions. For the good of the employees and staff, and the well-being of the company, a first-class business also depends on 'enjoying the experience'.

When I did sales, I had the chance to visit other companies and meet people in their own workplace, and it was obvious that many of them did not enjoy working. This lack of enthusiasm is summed up in a saying that always made me wince: "Thank God it's Friday." This attitude is widespread. Most people live for the time outside of work, especially the weekends. The idea that working itself can be nurturing and enjoyable is foreign to many people.

Of course it is possible to derive satisfaction from work through monetary rewards, seeing improvements in quality, productivity and efficiency, getting good results, or even from having a client paying early. But these are external sources of nourishment. The internal part is enjoying the experience of working itself. Working well generates a special feeling. If it feeds your energy back to you, it prevents burnout.

Appreciating Accomplishments

At Dharma Enterprises we tried various ways to help everyone develop and experience the joy of working. Usually at the end of the week or the completion of a project, we would make a list of achievements. Also, we kept a yearly timeline, recording events and accomplishments decorated with photographs and other illustrative material.

Inner enjoyment can begin with appreciating the opportunities that work offers. Another is seeing improvements taking shape. As individuals, we find joy in learning new skills and expanding responsibilities. At Dharma Enterprises we were gratified whenever the flow of work became more even and steady, or when we could make the workspace more attractive. Also we learned that it was wiser not to put too much emphasis on praise, but to focus instead on sensing and appreciating accomplishments for ourselves. Of course, acknowledging that someone has done a good job is inspiring in the short term. But too many compliments encourage a shift from valuing internal growth to relying on external rewards. When we depend upon the approval of others, we never seem to get enough. In fact, too much praise somehow robs us of the ability to appreciate our own efforts. Nourishment coming from outside cannot last, unless in some way it stirs up an internal process.

The real basis for the joy of working is being in contact with feelings. This is the inner side of work. You can learn to feel the flow of work: of timely interaction, of cooperation. Every situation has a feel to it—even the material and the job in itself. Recognition and appreciation stir up feelings, and interacting with the feeling tones recharges the activity of working. The dynamic interplay of all the forces at hand brings in a never-ending stream of vitality. In the middle of the stream, working is effortless, and knowledge on how to proceed becomes freely accessible. We are at one with our work. This feeling is the joy of working. It nurtures the heart and feeds the soul of the company, spreading the fragrance of success.

3

Bring the Dharma There

The organic link between work and spiritual values becomes clear as soon as we ask what it is that we really want out of life. At this fundamental level, there is really little difference between the business world and spiritual concerns.

Rinpoche's advice to meet our financial commitments and to become a first-class business affected us in our attitude and behavior. Yet his request to "bring the Dharma" to Dharma Enterprises resonated on a deeper level. For us, bringing the Dharma to our operations implied a heartfelt, direct connection with Tarthang Tulku and the lineage he represents. It was as if we had instantly become an extension of this lineage, like a small branch on an immense tree. Tiny sprout that we were, we could give form to what we loved.

The connection to Dharma turned the company into an adventure. Without Dharma, we would have had our Skillful Means practice, but in other respects we would have been little more than a rather ordinary noisy production plant in West Oakland. But with the Dharma connection, Dharma Enterprises became a special venture. The physical plant—the freshly painted building, snugly framed by boxes of flowers; the twenty flagpoles flying colored prayer flags on the roof, marking the location from afar; the name and logo of Dharma Enterprises in gold-painted letters on the building's exterior—hinted at this connection, and sealed the facilities.

The word Dharma refers to the teachings of the Buddha, the historical figure Siddhartha Gautama. The Buddha became fully enlightened, and his example proves that it is possible for human beings to awaken their potential. The very name 'Buddha' gives a clue for how to do this, since the Sanskrit term means 'Awakened One', and the Tibetan equivalent, 'sangs-rgyas', means 'everything negative gone, everything positive fully developed'. The Buddha showed us the way to achieve this, drawing out the best in ourselves in each situation. His teachings offer a myriad of means to do this. But the underlying message found in the Dharma is this: We are responsible for our own destiny. It is up to each one of us to make life meaningful. No one else can do it for us.

A central Dharma teaching is that human life is precious, and that we have limited time to make the most of it. A related teaching is that the restlessness and dissatisfaction we feel at times is our own doing. It comes about when we ignore the basic truth that everything is impermanent.

Rather than wasting time or getting stuck in often needless suffering, it is possible to cultivate the mind so that it becomes a beacon of light. Each of us, being on a journey in time, has a mission to make the best of this life, especially considering the long-term effects of our actions today.

These insights have the special flavor of the Dharma. They are like a key that opens the door to what is true, independent of our specific circumstances in time and space. At Dharma Enterprises we were intent on making our work a Dharma practice. We saw clearly, through our familiarity with the principles of Skillful Means, that work offers the opportunity to develop the mind. We realized that a creative enterprise can foster integrity and dignity. Nourished by this glimmer of light, we could in turn feed other Dharma projects, thus keeping in motion a cycle of positive accomplishments.

The business of printing has many special connections to the Dharma. Historically, Dharma Press had learned the art of printing in order to publish Buddhist books and art reproductions. Once printing skills were developed, it was natural to look for commercial printing business to financially support the publishing activity. The activity of printing, performed to the steady rhythms of the presses, stimulates physical energy, while producing high-quality products demands concentration and an excellent eye. Just as baking bread can be a noble profession because it feeds the body, the craft of printing can nourish the soul. By stimulating and refining energy, and developing concentration and precision, it provides excellent support for a well-rounded human education.

These factors were especially important to us because although we continued to print the literature of ancient wisdom, the majority of the work we did was strictly commercial, for customers such as the phone company, banks, and the software industry. This meant that we often produced advertising materials. Yet we were free to continue our Dharma practice by cultivating skills, energy, and caring, so helpful for integrating body and mind.

The inner essence of Dharma practice is called Skillful Means. If Dharma is the inner wisdom, Skillful Means is the application—wisdom in action. It is a general principle of Dharma that the awakening of potential takes place through body, speech, and mind. Therefore, Skillful Means stresses that it is possible to refine the way we think, speak, and act, thus giving more meaning to our actions. The methods of Skillful Means help us to recognize the truth of our intrinsic freedom, and express it in our daily life.

Creating a Dharma Center

It was a challenge to create a work environment and a production facility that Rinpoche and his lama friends would recognize as a Dharma center. To avoid alienating any of our customers, we decided to place most of the sacred images and symbols we kept at Dharma Enterprises in a private room. It contained an altar, pictures of the Nyingma lineage, and a magnificent prayer wheel that turned continuously, turning out over 700 million prayers per day. As soon as the prayer wheel was installed, it felt as if a living Buddha had entered the building. The prayer wheel and its steady hum became a symbol for our ways of working, establishing a dynamic energy to spread the Dharma around the clock.

Other signs of the Dharma were visible to anyone dealing with us. On the pressroom wall we mounted a quilted panel displaying two dragons, measuring about ten by forty feet. In the center of the room hung a multi-colored victory banner. At the other end of the work space, colored panels embroidered with the Dharma Enterprises' logo hung from the ceiling to the floor. On the roof of the building there were the ever-waving prayer flags, mostly in red and yellow, with images and sacred texts. The flags were replaced as soon as they began to fray, having done their work of sending good wishes to all beings. Sometimes customers would ask about their significance, and when we explained that the flags were intended to bring universal blessings, they were often touched, becoming still. The company's logo, the moon rising from a lotus, which reflected the unification of wisdom and action, was also a Dharma symbol, designed by Rinpoche in response to our request.

Apart from displaying these various Dharma symbols, we decided not to lay out specific rules for how to be a Dharma center. We knew that this would come naturally if we diligently practiced Skillful Means and did what we could to help Dharma Press in printing their own publications.

Right Livelihood

Traditionally, in Tibet, a functioning Dharma center such as a monastery with its college and retreat centers would enjoy the financial support of the entire surrounding region. In America this is not the case, and nowadays Dharma activity needs to be self-sufficient. Production of the texts, sacred images, and symbols that promote wisdom depends on a money-generating source. That is one reason our community developed the idea of operating commercial enterprises. Dharma Enterprises was the principal example of this approach.

Working for Dharma Enterprises let us make a living, practice the Dharma, and at the same time work for a good cause. This is consistent with the Buddhist teaching called 'right livelihood'. The word 'right' here refers to 'complete', which means in part working for yourself and others at the same time—not only for others, and not only for yourself.

The Skillful Means principles aim to stimulate right livelihood in any activity, providing it is not harmful or destructive to the spirit. This way of working and living is possible in any situation, whether in a publishing house, an oil refinery, or a television production company. In each situation you have the option to consider the long-term benefits of the enterprise for others and for the society as a whole. As long as the adage of benefit for both self and others is kept in mind, and brought into play in making long-term policy and in the day-to-day approach, it will nurture the natural longing to live in accord with 'right livelihood'.

Right livelihood is a high principle in the Dharma. It invites us to live in accord with the wisdom of an awakened mind. How can we develop this idea in daily life? Over the years Rinpoche often stressed that it is helpful to look at the effect of our actions on our own minds. He would say, "Make sure that you do not cause any suffering to yourself. Every time you are emotional you undermine yourself. With lack of trust and feelings of guilt you harm yourself and therefore others. Try to heal your own minds. That is the best you can offer."

This emphasis on healing the mind became an important principle at Dharma Enterprises. Spurred on to be aware of how our actions affected our inner state of mind, we practiced right livelihood by putting love and wisdom into what we were doing, moment to moment. It might begin with picking up a piece of paper from the floor or making a helpful gesture to a co-worker. Gradually caring became the norm and love became the form.

The practice of Skillful Means in this sense is linked to religion in the original sense of the word. The Latin word 'religio' means 'to bind'. Life and work became our religion as we put love into what we believed in. Bound by love, our ways of working gained a spiritual dimension. Creative action became the ritual, and invoking knowledge became the ceremony. The stillness of silent awareness and the overarching vision of the enterprise became our prayer. In taking responsibility we gave free reign to the knowledge of the heart, empowering ourselves with a wisdom not separate from the wisdom of ancient traditions.

All Work is Dharma Work

The first employees and managers at Dharma Enterprises had all been studying Dharma teachings for some time. The idea of working for a commercial enterprise while practicing Skillful Means as the daily application of Dharma at work was intriguing and exciting.

This shared intention had a bonding effect, encouraging us to work together rather than pursue individual concerns. What was good for the whole would be good for each of us, and also for the clients we planned to serve. We took as our motto, "do what is good for Dharma Enterprises," and we decided to practice it through the three basic commitments we had made: a first-class business, meeting our financial commitments, and practicing the Dharma. All this was fundamental to a more formal training in Skillful Means management. It was several years before such training actually began.

Bringing this clear vision to life was not that simple. Tensions emerged now and then, but we learned that if we let our decisions be guided by the good of Dharma Enterprises, we could quickly find a common meeting ground. Working on this basis was uplifting. It became like an elixir to the company. Focusing on the good of the organization let us unite our energy and our minds, and in this way we gradually created the heart of the enterprise.

This transition from the individual to the whole, from personal likes and dislikes into an "open" style of working, would take many years. When it did begin to manifest, it was deeply rewarding. Even if flare-ups occurred, they did not prevent anyone from cooperating wholeheartedly a few minutes later. In addition to seeing the financial results of our work, this deeper level of cooperation made our work enjoyable. It kindled in us a respect for ourselves and for others.

An important element in all this was the commitment we made right from the beginning to make no distinction between commercial work and the printing of Dharma books. We did not forget that the commercial work brought in the money that made it possible to publish Dharma materials. So commercial work was Dharma work too. Acting on this intent encouraged us to develop precisely the qualities necessary for both commercial work and Dharma practice: caring, imagination, quality, precision and punctuality. The organization needed us to merge work and practice, and this motto made it very clear: All our work is Dharma work!

Managing with Skillful Means

Two years went by before we implemented a structured Skillful Means practice. Why did it take us so long? First of all, we had to learn the business. Printing is a complicated craft, and the market is demanding. Also, the company was growing fast, and we were constantly racing around to make it all work. We had to learn many things all at once: We were swimming in deep waters.

It need not be difficult to set up a Skillful Means training even in the first few weeks of a company's existence. What problems do you encounter and what potential do you want to cultivate in work? Take a look at the table of contents and the index of Tarthang Tulku's books *Skillful Means* and *Mastering Successful Work,* and one of the chapters or paragraphs undoubtedly will address your interest. You can start right there, reading the text, practicing what is suggested and evaluating for yourself the effects of your efforts.

In our case we did not begin in this obvious way. Instead we started by developing visualization. Perhaps this is because we did so much physical work. We needed a mental image, like a greater vision directing our best intentions and raw energy. We tried various kinds of visualizations to steady the mind so that our work became even, with heightened concentration.

Only after about two years of practicing in this way did we establish regular seminar-like meetings and start to take different topics from Rinpoche's books and the manuals we had been provided. At the same time, we instituted individual meetings, encouraging each other to practice more diligently and to see through recurring obstacles. Gradually a balance was found between action and reflection, integrating the topics we were studying into our daily work. Again and again we realized that work is practice—work is our personal wisdom in action. Through our work we make our imprints upon time.

At various stages, and especially when we focused on studying the topic of time, Rinpoche engaged us in lively exchanges. We also received a steady stream of manuals and informal suggestions to help us to make Skillful Means the pivot of our work. Carefully studying theory and practice, we saw the momentum of right livelihood take form, and saw how the Skillful Means teachings offered a road map to success. Through Skillful Means Management Training the company and the employees could shape the soul of the company.

The essence of Skillful Means training is developing awareness and taking responsibility against the background of time. As we developed more awareness, a subtle, gentle transition occurred from 'me' to 'us', from 'what can I get' to 'how can I help' and then to 'what needs to be done'. We became less preoccupied with ourselves, and realized that in the long run the emotions we experienced from day to day did not really matter. In a year or even a month from now, we would not recall how we felt today. What endured was what we did and the results we created together. Only "doing what is good for Dharma Enterprises" counted.

Helping Dharma Press

From the first day that Dharma Enterprises began, we knew that ours was a temporary existence. We had emerged from Dharma Press, and knew that eventually we would return to Dharma Press. We were merely a temporary blossom on a growing tree. But while we were in operation, we were able to help Dharma Press with its thousands of books and hundreds of thousands of sacred art reproductions. Because our equipment was state of the art, we could refine the work being produced so that it became truly exquisite.

Over the eleven years of our existence we printed about 650 jobs for Dharma Press. About once a week we would produce a book, a catalogue, or a set of sacred art posters. We were fortunate enough to reprint a tiny part of the Kanjur and Tanjur (the spoken word of the Buddha and its commentaries), and briefly helped to assemble the Great Treasures of Ancient Teachings (the extant texts and commentaries of the Nyingma School of Tibetan Buddhism, and major works of other schools). These two sets together amount to over 780 volumes, ranging far and wide into disciplines such as philosophy, psychology, medicine, logic, astronomy, astrology, ritual, and art. Buddhism is truly a path of knowledge. Although we did not produce most of the actual books, the royalties we paid contributed primarily to the formidable costs of manufacturing these sets.

It took many years and demanded great financial resources to put together these books of wisdom, made with the intention to last at least three hundred years. One of our final gestures before the flame of Dharma Enterprises was extinguished in 1998 was the purchase on behalf of Dharma Press of a new two-color forty-inch Heidelberg Press. In this way we knew that Dharma Press would have the means to continue its good work, while continuing to implement and develop Skillful Means Management Training. Although Dharma Enterprises is gone, Dharma Press is alive and well today. May it continue to benefit all beings for a long time to come.

Practice of Skillful Means

1st-Class Business
Body   action, profits, results
           (meeting financial commitments)
Speech service, being on time (Skillful Means)
Mind   attitude, quality (1st-class vision)

Bring the Dharma: What is good for the whole
Body   manuals, guidelines, classes (1st-class setup)
Speech regular practice (Skillful Means)
Mind   benefitting the Dharma
           (meeting financial commitments)

Meeting Financial Commitments
Body   paying the bills, commitment (1st-class)
Speech not missing payments; paying on time
           (Skillful Means)
Mind   benefitting the Dharma
           (meeting financial commitments)

Challenging Abilities
Body   learning new skills (Cooperation)
Speech bringing people together (Communication)
Mind   developing positive knowledge (Responsibility)

Overcoming Obstacles
Body   overcoming aversion, laziness ("just do it")
Speech overcoming grasping, anxiety ("5% more")
Mind   overcoming ignorance, confusion
           ("getting results")

Transforming Negativity
Body   overcoming resistance (learn to care)
Speech overcoming resentment (develop joy in
           one's own and others' accomplishments)
Mind   overcoming despair (faith in relationship
           between action and result)

Vision–Path–Goals

PART TWO

Skillful Means

4

Wisdom in Action

*With our head, our heart, and our guts united, we can
accomplish something meaningful for ourselves and beneficial for
others, and enjoy a steady stream of understanding and insight.
This is a skillful means way of uniting wisdom and compassion:
the Dharma in action for the modern world.*

When I was just becoming interested in Buddhism,
I read something that I later realized was based
on the first verse of the Dhammapada, one of the
Buddha's most important teachings. It said: *We are who
we think we are, having become who we thought we were.*

By taking hold of the power of mind, we can change
our ways of being in the world. Therefore, analyzing
and training the mind is crucial. What wisdom informs
our actions? How can we skillfully liberate each situation from unnecessary tension? How can we transform
the ordinary mind to awakened mind? To realize the
potential of the mind that is within each of us, it is said
that the Buddha has taught 84,000 topics.

At the heart of these teachings are the six 'paramitas', activities and qualities that can bring about this profound change in us. The meaning of the word paramita refers to 'going to the other shore', passing from ordinary mind to wakefulness. The paramitas, or transcending functions, both lead to and express awakened mind. By applying the paramitas, we will gradually become wiser and act in increasingly appropriate ways.

The six paramitas are generosity, discipline, patience, effort, concentration, and, finally, wisdom. The first five paramitas refer to the activity of *doing*, leading to wisdom. The last paramita, wisdom, refers to the activity of *mind*, refining all our actions. Together, the six paramitas are said to be like the two wings of a bird, giving the power to live in freedom and act wisely. They are called skillful means, representing wisdom in action, practices to develop wisdom and caring in daily life.

Although traditionally the teachings of the Buddha were largely explored in a monastic setting, the six paramitas are intended for everyone. Anyone can practice skillful means, at any time and any place. All we need to do is aim for the 'right' action—action that is complete, takes everything into consideration, and aims to draw out the best in each situation.

Action is a most valuable teacher. We learn by doing. The more we understand, the more suitable our actions will become. Knowledge and action feed each other, in a cycle of perpetual motion. Knowledge without action is a waste, while action without knowledge inevitably creates confusion. But when action and knowledge interact dynamically, they make a perfect couple, joined together by skillful means.

Introducing this principle—that true wisdom may be developed through action—has been one of Tarthang Tulku's great contributions to the West. He offers a great variety of means to make daily life, and especially work, more enjoyable and effective. He has called these materials, founded on the paramitas, 'Skillful Means'—referring to *learning through action*.

The Paramitas

For over 2500 years in the Buddhist teachings, the six paramitas have been the core of the quest for higher wisdom in daily life. They are the means to attain enlightenment, and all the great teachers of Tibet have emphasized that these activities direct our energy away from emotionality and confusion toward integrity, dignity, and stability.

Generosity Gives Enjoyment

Generosity means giving freely, without holding back, fully participating with all your energy and intelligence. It is the antidote to avarice and greed. Being generous also means sharing knowledge. Instead of withholding or resisting, you can give to the situation you find yourself in, to whatever needs to be done.

Generosity can be acquired: You can learn to be more generous by starting with small acts of giving. You may make a point of noticing what needs to be done, what contribution you can make. You can ask questions: How can I help? When you participate fully, without regrets for the past or anxiety about the future, generosity begins to grow. In being generous, you recapture the joy of being.

Discipline Brings Happiness

While generosity fuels aliveness, discipline gives it form. Through discipline you shape what you love. It is an antidote to aversion. Practicing discipline will set the stage to draw out your potential. In developing a discipline you become a 'disciple' of the meaning of your life. It enables you to concentrate on what works for you, and stop doing what does not work. For discipline to be complete, and to provide reliable results, it should involve body, speech, and mind. In other words, you must become aware and take hold of your attitudes and your thoughts, of what you say and what you do, and then take action accordingly.

In the context of work, discipline means being dependable and reliable—keeping your promises. Discipline is related to time: being on time, knowing what you do with your time, what you wish to accomplish in time, and ultimately, what you wish to leave behind over time. Discipline helps to shape what really matters. Seeing your aspirations come to life brings happiness.

Patience Draws Out Beauty

Patience requires staying with what you are doing, rather than giving in to restlessness or compulsive behavior. It is an antidote to anger. Patience is always being ready, able to capture what is valuable. In being patient you become open to others and to each situation. Letting go of opinions and judgments makes you more sensitive to timing, able to proceed at the right pace, neither too slow nor too fast. Patience leads away from the periphery into the center of experience, where you find appreciation and beauty.

Patience allows everything to come into focus. You can apply yourself entirely, not just with your attention, but with all your senses open. As you persist, new opportunities reveal themselves. You sense when the time is right, and your activity becomes a work of art.

Effort Produces Splendor

While patience discovers what is good, effort brings it into being. Effort means never giving up. It counters laziness and kindles aliveness. When you remember that time is precious, effort prevents you from wasting it.

How can you develop effort? Start by developing a discipline of effort. Set targets and goals related to time. Learn about your tendencies to hold back and wait, and be generous with your energy instead. As you become familiar with your energy, you will get a taste of your own strength. Encourage yourself patiently. Effort may merely be a matter of 'more' or 'longer', but usually it is about 'better'—better communication, better cooperation, better results, and a better use of time. Effort is applied passion. As it gains momentum, integrating what was formerly separate, each situation sparkles with splendor, and working becomes increasingly effortless.

Concentration Leads to Peace of Mind

To align yourself with what you are doing right now, without giving in to distractions, is the beginning of concentration. At first concentration may require squeezing your attention tightly, but gradually you learn to establish a light focus. Concentration counters grasping and anxiety. Extended concentration can only be supported by an ongoing relaxation in the body and mind. In the process you become calmer and clearer.

Like the other paramitas, concentration includes all six paramitas. It depends on being generously involved with body and mind. To establish a steady concentration, you will need to encourage yourself to set a discipline, and to practice patience and effort as well. Then concentration will penetrate obstacles and reveal the most reliable road to success.

To practice concentration at work, begin by paying attention and developing mindfulness about what is needed and by when. As you also develop sensitivity to the quality of your concentration, you will naturally assemble what is required to finish the task at hand. Your concentration will bundle your energy and mind as you refine how you work.

With concentration you come into time, linking it with awareness. Past and future dissolve in the present moment, your mind is at peace, and you are open to embody wisdom, the sixth paramita.

Wisdom Recaptures Freedom

In the teachings of the Buddha wisdom is a most profound principle. It includes but goes beyond conceptual understanding and involves knowledge of every kind. The paramita of wisdom counters not-knowing, confusion, and most basically, lack of awareness. Since awareness and being are inseparable, the more awareness the lighter, stronger, and wiser your being.

There are a great many ways to develop wisdom. In the business context, you can begin through learning skills and improving the usage of time. As soon as you understand how something works there is a sense of relief—now you know how to do it. Learning from your actions is empowering. As you learn from your mistakes and face the results of your actions, your resolve is strengthened, providing a solid base for improvement.

Business has its own intelligence and wisdom. It often begins with common sense, 'street smarts', and being savvy. Learning about people, about time, about how money works, and about producing quality may sometimes be disillusioning, but such knowledges become the pillars of success.

In order to develop this kind of understanding you have to muster up interest and be able to sustain it. You may be interested because you are worried or afraid or because you are determined to make something happen—in any case, what counts is that you want to know something. On that basis you can learn to be sharp in

61

your observations and analysis, and to question issues and potentialities.

There are times when you understand more than you actually show in daily life. You are not backing up your understanding with energy and so are not able to embody your wisdom. When you realize your wisdom is lacking energy, the first five paramitas can help give the power to enact knowledge. They help you to step into the world and produce or manifest what you know is right over time.

The six paramitas function as a map, a guide for behavior and a strategy for how to work well. For example, if you find that joy or happiness are missing from your life, you can practice generosity or discipline. Likewise, beauty emerges with patience, and aliveness with effort. As your concentration and commitment deepen, a steady peace of mind appears. Exercising knowledge leads to wisdom. In the end, it is wisdom that will set you free to attain the highest success.

The Paramitas in Business

When exploring the effects of the paramitas, work with the paramita of your choice. You will soon find the others are involved too. The six paramitas all feed back into each other in ways that apply directly to business concerns. Efficiency improves with discipline. Patience prepares you for opportunities. Productivity depends on effort, and concentration assures quality. The more generous you are, the more helpful you will be and the more you enjoy what you do. With knowledge you

Obstacle	Paramita	Action
holding back	generosity	participating fully
postponing	discipline	being dedicated
avoiding	patience	being ready
giving up	effort	giving 5% more
going away	concentration	focusing more
making mistakes	wisdom	aiming for lasting results

regain the freedom to be creative and aim for the highest accomplishments.

Sharing Knowledge

Sharing knowledge is an integral aspect of Skillful Means. When an entire company practices Skillful Means, knowledge will spread throughout the organization like blood circulating throughout the body. The head informs the heart, and gut energy becomes aligned with vision. Each constantly informs the others of how to function best. This circulation stimulates collective intelligence and develops the inner resources of both the individuals and the organization. Sharing knowledge encourages respect, friendship, and leadership and stimulates growth. Learning, acting, and sharing feed and merge into one another. They create a tapestry of Skillful Means—Wisdom in Action.

In the chapters that follow, I have chosen a few topics from the vast range of Skillful Means subjects presented in Tarthang Tulku's books *Skillful Means* and *Mastering Successful Work*. These topics were practiced intensively during the ten years of Skillful Means at Dharma Enterprises. If you scrutinize them carefully, you will recognize that the six paramitas are fully integrated into each topic. Whether the focus is studying the value of time, developing positive knowledge, or taking responsibility, the importance of generosity, discipline, patience, effort, and concentration is easy to detect. You will discover that you already have the knowledge to be successful. To activate this knowledge is the inner practice of Skillful Means.

5

Mastering Time

*With the power of time on our side,
each one of us can be a hero.*

Each breath you take gives you more time to live.
When you breathe out for the last time, your life
has come to an end. Time is the active force and the
substance of life; in fact, time is all you have. This is
your life. Your life is the time you have. The time is now.

To enter time, you must go through four gates. At
the first gate you have to let go of the past. Being completely involved with what you are doing helps you
through the second gate. The third gate will open when
you are no longer pulled toward the future. Finally,
when you shed the sense of 'I', you pass through the
fourth and last gate. Now you enter time.

Discovering Time

When we set up a Skillful Means training, it was not
immediately obvious what would be the best way to pro-

ceed. The ideal formula had to be discovered over the years. Gradually we instituted regular seminar-like meetings, individual meetings, readings, discussions, and specific weekly practices. In time we found a balance between action and reflection, and created ways to integrate the topics we were studying into our work. We constantly encouraged each other to remember that work is practice, our personal wisdom in action. Knowing we could learn as we went along, we began to fine-tune our inner resources.

One of our first topics was the brief chapter on time in Tarthang Tulku's book *Skillful Means,* which focuses on the nature of time, the value of time, and the energy of time. At first these topics seemed lofty and out of reach. It was not easy to figure out what time was about. Theoretically we understood that the nature of time is reflected in impermanence. We were familiar with deadlines, and with how the value of time manifested itself clearly when a deadline was strict; then each hour, each minute counted. Beyond that, we did not have much sense of the value of our time, unless value referred to making sure to 'have a good time'. As to what the 'energy of time' might mean, we did not have a clue. Yet somehow these ideas spoke to us. We knew we were on to something.

A few years later, we started on a second round of working with the concepts of time. By then we had developed a more concrete approach. Each work day was broken up into two-hour increments. At the end of each segment we stopped for a minute to record what we had actually done during that time.

Our experience surprised us. By becoming aware of time in this way, we found there was enough time to do everything we had planned, and even more. We started to use our time better, and anxieties about not finishing on time disappeared into the background. Being engaged in time prevented emotions from taking hold, making us feel more free. Working became less stressful. The effect was exhilarating. Bringing time into awareness seemed to have an empowering effect. Was this perhaps the 'energy of time' that we were somehow connecting to? We had no definite answers, but we felt we had discovered Time.

During this period, something almost palpable was happening. Right at this time Tarthang Tulku asked us what topics we were studying. It was as though he could sense the shift. When we responded with written papers, he quickly gave new suggestions in the form of a paper entitled 'Waking up to Time'. This new material presented marvelous insights. Until then, our efforts had focused on awareness of time, but now we began to explore the idea that we might be able to control time, even master it. We knew that deadlines could stimulate energy, concentration, and creativity. But now we were taking time to heart. We began to learn to connect to time with body, mind, and soul.

Time's Pressure

People usually spend much of their time fretting about the past: inner dialogues, regrets, and dreams of how things might have been. Or they are caught up in anxiety about the future: making plans, hoping, and fearing. Lost in the past, worrying about the future, or holding back—in any of these states of mind you are bound to feel incomplete. You are cast 'out' of time, alienated from its flow. Time seems to be passing you by. Experiencing time as a monster, being dissatisfied with how you spend your time, or always feeling rushed and in a hurry are all indicators of being 'out' of time. Consider these emotions as a signal, a wake-up call: You are no longer connected to time.

Still, there are moments when you are not so preoccupied and scattered. Suppose you are saying farewell to someone you love. In the few moments remaining, you somehow manage to find the perfect expression for your deepest feelings. Spending time with someone who is facing death, you are engaged with your whole being. Despite the fact that you are witnessing the end of a phase, even of a life, there is a precious intimacy in the air. Time is rich and full; a minute can be an eternity. You are most alive.

At work you feel a similar sense of intimate aliveness when everyone involved embraces a deadline wholeheartedly. If only this intimacy could be felt all the time! Your actions and your relationships would become infinitely more dynamic and nourishing.

At Dharma Enterprises the best times we had were when we worked under great pressure. The moment the art work for a rush project arrived, all departments would swing into action. There were no gaps in communication, concentration was high, and cooperation flowed perfectly. Everybody was tuned in. These kinds of emergencies gave us the opportunity to show our caring and get a good taste of time.

Time's Power

When you are totally present, something powerful happens. Time is full and seems to slow down. It is as if you are pulled into time. You cherish the uniqueness of each moment, knowing it cannot last. Your eyes are opened wide; all the senses are awake. You embrace time fully. Like plugging in an appliance to produce power or light, you connect with time's vitality.

The conflicts you encounter in day-to-day life may actually be a sign that you are not 'in' time. When time is not central in your life, you experience it as an outside force bearing down on you, and therefore much energy is wasted on catching up with time. There is never enough time. If only there were thirty-six hours in the day, or if you had four hands instead of two! But as it is, you have no way to handle time's pressure.

In your mind, time may be a spoilsport. It flies when you are having fun and stops when you are anxious for it to pass. When you are impatiently watching the clock, five minutes seem like an eternity. And when you want to hold on to the present moment, it slips through your fingers. It is impossible to get a grip on time. But all this takes time too lightly. There is more to time than what is reflected by the ticking of the clock.

As you start to become aware of time, it will gradually become a part of you. Try seeing what happens if you let go of any preoccupation with yourself and instead make time your focus. You may be surprised at time's flexibility. If you cherish and respect time as an ally, a generous friend, you may gain access to an abundance of time. When you bring time to awareness, it will become the greater theme in your life.

Waking Up to Time

Time was here before you were born, and time will be here after you die. In between birth and death, you are living on borrowed time. Yet time's dynamic energy is always with you. You can become familiar with it, enabling its power to reveal itself. Its immediacy is reflected in the beating of your heart. Listen to your heart, and you will discover time's nature, value, and energy. Knowing these qualities of time intimately will enable you to make the best use of your time.

The Nature of Time

The nature of time is that it passes. Time's flow makes all things impermanent: What begins will inevitably come to an end; what comes together will certainly fall apart. Time itself stays, but your time is limited. Each moment is unique: There is no such thing as a second chance. It is the nature of time that opportunities do not last. On the other hand, time is open and generous—anything can happen. Here on the threshold of the present, the future is open and possibilities are infinite.

In our daily work we encouraged each other to remember that time passes, that in fact it was running out. This helped us prepare for what would come next, whether it was new print orders or getting invoices out on time. With awareness of the nature of time we also saw the need to bring a project to a good end. It was never too late to participate in the way we might have wanted to all along.

As time changes, each moment offers an opportunity to start over again, and in taking it you heal the past. With mindfulness of the nature of time, moment to moment, cycle to cycle, awareness has fewer gaps or lapses, and there are fewer abrupt transitions. There are no surprises; you are prepared for things to come.

The Value of Time

Time is short, and therefore all the more precious. The value of time is that it can be used. Time is at your disposal, and you can decide what to do with it. You can set your own standards and targets. Those who are not paid by the hour, like a lawyer, may tend to disregard the value of their time and that of others. For us the value of time became obvious when a job was spoiled and we had to muster up the necessary concentration, energy, and care to compensate for the mistake. When we did use time well, each one of us could sense the joy of having a good time. Appreciating time's value is the key to enjoyment.

The Energy of Time

Everything has a deadline: this job, this project, this day. You too are living on a deadline. Acknowledging this fact may give you a charge. This is the energy of time. The business world with its demands on time and quality is a perfect arena to draw out the energy of time. Embracing the knowledge that time is at a premium makes you want to stop wasting it. How you act right now is important. As your awareness merges with time's energy, your intentions become clear and your actions more succinct and prompt. You may feel the urge to bypass the irrelevant, or to avoid duplication and go right to the heart of the matter. You are tapping the energy of time.

Anyone who works with machines has an opportunity to learn about deadlines and about connecting to the energy of time. An idle machine like a big press or folder is almost eerie, but when it runs smoothly and evenly, its humming sound is soothing. At our company we had a machine that bound paperback books. The machine operator put the collated pages into a pocket, and the machine then cut off a sliver along the spine, applied glue and wrapped the cover around the book. This binder had five pockets moving in a circle. One day it was my job to put the pages neatly into the pockets and after they had been glued, stack the finished books. Meanwhile the next pocket would show up, ready to be filled. There was no choice but to tune in and align hands, eyes, and energy with the rhythm of the moving pockets. A missed pocket is not a disaster, but an opportunity is lost. Fine-tuning my movements was energizing and, as my work improved, the movements became like a dance. When the job was finished, done right and on time, I felt almost blissful.

Out of Time

Bringing time to the foreground may reveal how often you are unaware of time. Part of the problem is that you are usually more concerned with your 'self' than with time. This means that you spend much of your time dwelling in the past or future. It may seem as if time just does not play a vital role. But the real problem is that you are not present. When you slide off into the past or future, it is like leaving the freeway and turning into a dead-end street. Momentarily you may sense a disconnection or a loss, dominated by a feeling of disease and negativity. These are signs that you are cut off from time. You are no longer 'in' time.

When you feel dark, dull, and heavy, or basically stuck, you are probably 'out' of time. You experience a sense of isolation, and the slightest activity requires effort. You are unaware of the nature, value, and energy of time. Being out of time manifests in three ways:

Being a victim of time   When you ignore the nature of time, you find yourself wondering where your time has gone. All you know is that it is 'too late'. Time has passed, and you are unprepared for what is to come. You may feel altogether worthless, even despairing, not knowing what to do next. The remedy is to stop ignoring time—to wake up to time.

Being short of time   When you are anxious about things to come, you fail to recognize the value of 'this' time. You find yourself grasping for more. Always living in the future, you fear being somehow left out or worry about not having enough time. Not taking advantage of the present, you naturally feel short of time. Since this moment, now, has been pawned to the future, you cannot appreciate or enjoy its value. Since you have not used 'this' time well, you are likely to feel resentful or guilty; you may look for someone to blame. The remedy is to stop grasping and take control of time now.

Wasting time   When you refuse to participate in the action going on around you, you are in fact resisting the energy of time. You cannot possibly be ignited or nourished by it. Out of resistance or aversion, you hold back your energy. You let time pass by, hoping things will get better by themselves. Feeling dissatisfied, you find yourself thinking 'I am sick and tired of it'. The remedy is to stop aversion and participate in the energy of what is going on.

You may recognize yourself in all three of these patterns. How can you turn around this lack of awareness of one of the most precious resources available to human beings? It is easy enough to say, 'stop ignoring', 'stop grasping', and 'stop aversion', but what can you do? The table on the following page may help you to explore the steps that would lead in the right direction.

Using Time

Time is not just the background against which your days unfold. It actually makes up the entire fabric of

Out of Time	In Time
Dis-ease	At ease
Isolation	Intimacy
Incompletion, emptiness	Wholeness, contentment
Fear	Faith and confidence
Suffering	Appropriate action
Missing opportunities	Taking opportunities
Renouncing responsibility	Taking responsibility
Prisoner of emotions	Freedom
Wasting potential	Waking up to potential
Procrastinating	Participating
Pale, heavy, dark	Bright, light, open
Depression	Love of life
Failure	Success
Abnormal	Normal

Ignoring Time

Victim of time, Feeling worthless	By taking responsibility, you gain meaning

Grasping Time

Short of time, feeling resentful	By focusing, you gain joy

Aversion to Time

Waste of time, feeling dissatisfied	By giving, you gain satisfaction

life. Coming back into time begins with waking up to it, bringing time to awareness and awareness to time. You can invite time into your life, letting it wake up in your mind just as the sun rises in the morning. A practical way to wake up to time is to become aware of how you have used it.

At our company we did this through a four-month program. During the *first month,* start by making a daily schedule, breaking the day down into two-hour segments. Every two hours, write down in five words or less what you just did, without guilt or blame. Stay away from judgments or labels. Just note the facts.

Keeping a log of how you use your time may not hold any immediate attraction for you, but do not accept this resistance. Remember that anything outside the scope of your habits feels unfamiliar and burdensome at first. Resistance means that you have come up against a wall of unawareness that impedes the sparkle of time from entering your being. Pay no attention; take on the challenge. For about two weeks, do not even give yourself a choice: Simply go ahead and report how you have used your time. Once the resistance has ebbed away, it will be exhilarating to continue for another two weeks.

As long as you are unaware of time, you are at a loss about where it went. You will have a few memories, but in general the past will be foggy and inaccessible. Recording how you use your time will help. You will not necessarily be able to recall all the facts and details, but the practice will remove the dead weight of history.

From now on, the present will hold awareness of the past. The gaps between then and now diminish.

As soon as the daily schedule becomes a part of your life, it begins to produce results. Every two hours you get a 'wake-up call', since you have to write down what you just did. Knowing that you will soon have to report back to yourself on whether you made the most of the time will make you more alert. The hours ahead may seem more open. Not only will you feel as though there is more time, but you will be determined to use it well.

In the *second month*, add a positive thought at the start of each day, a phrase or word you would like to bear in mind that provides an overarching vision for that day. It could be anything from 'find new clients' or 'be more patient' to 'improve the work flow'. Every day is imbued with a new idea, a fresh perspective.

This positive thought will prevent you from merely reacting to whatever comes your way. Like most people, you probably spend too much time at work dealing with surprise situations or putting out fires. The positive intention of a guiding thought will give direction to your actions and let you take advantage of the opportunities the day presents. After one week, add a second positive thought, then a third. When you are working with three thoughts at once, make the first thought beneficial for the company, the second one that you simply enjoy, and the third a thought that is 'new' to you, opening up a fresh area. These three guides are like torches casting light ahead into the future. As you keep them in the back of your mind, time begins to unfold in harmony with them.

In the *third month,* you are ready to extend the schedule and take more control of time. Now you are more awake to time, and you are ready to take charge. Divide the page into two columns: In the right-hand column continue the practice of writing down what you have done every two hours, in a few neutral words; in the left-hand column begin planning the day, again in two-hour segments.

In the beginning, there is likely to be a discrepancy between what you plan and what you accomplish, but this does not matter. As the planning of the day expands and deepens, the two columns of your schedule will gradually become integrated, without any special effort on your part. As awareness of time expands, you will sense more time and feel less rushed. You are likely to accomplish more than you planned or even imagined. Life is flowing through you more freely. You are re-entering time, recapturing the energy you previously kept at bay. You are heading 'home'.

During the *fourth month,* add to the three positive thoughts and the two columns of the schedule a review of the day. After work is finished, reflect on your accomplishments. This will give you a sense of joy that enables you to retain the vitality of your actions. In this way work can recharge you. While looking back, acknowledge any negative actions you may have done, and decide on the changes you want to make tomorrow. This will prevent a rigid separation between one

Waking Up to Time

day/month/year

Three positive thoughts to develop today:

1.

2.

3.

Time	Planned	Accomplished
6–8 AM		
8–10		
10–12		
12–2 PM		
2–4		
4–6		
6–8		
8–10		

At the end of the day:

Reflect on what you have done.

Appreciate positive accomplishments.

Resolve to change.

Dedicate all positive actions.

day and the next, letting you enter a continuing stream of time, with fewer and fewer sharp transitions. Finally, you may wish to dedicate the benefits of your actions to a worthwhile cause, person or group of people. For example: "May all my positive actions today be dedicated to the benefit of the company, and to everyone involved with it." Such a dedication places a seal on your positive actions, and preserves all that has been valuable that day.

Working well, 'having a good time', is an indication of being 'in time'. You find yourself embracing deadlines. Giving everything you have merges time and awareness. You discover that the energy of time recharges you while you work. You are in your element.

Of course, such positive feelings do not last forever. Sooner or later you are bound to come out of the flow of time. As soon as you start rationalizing, or when a gap appears between one activity and the next, you are out of time again. It may seem as if you have to start all over again, but none of your efforts are really wasted: They all add up. Consider your work as a training ground for becoming familiar with yourself in time, and you will experience each moment as a rich opportunity.

Taking Control of Time

Waking up to time is like seeing a beautiful horse roaming in a meadow. Marveling at its beauty and power, you may long to ride it. Taking control of time is like preparing the horse and placing a saddle on its back.

Once in the saddle, you can ride away, leading it skillfully wherever you wish to go.

Taking control of time originates in recognizing the value of time and acting on this knowledge. Skillful Means offers a variety of ways to do this. Each method begins with a commitment to be on time, for this is the key to the gates of time. Starting and ending on time makes things lighter. If you start 'behind' time, you can never really catch up. Being late weighs on people—if not on yourself, then certainly on others. When ten people have a meeting and one person is five minutes late, the group has just lost forty-five minutes. Starting on time is tuning in to time, like an orchestra that starts together, all attuned to the same moment. Being on time makes everything fresh and dynamic.

Besides starting on time, we practiced three specific methods for making sure that time did not slip through our fingers. In a way they are shortcuts to taking control of time. They are: Challenging your abilities, overcoming obstacles, and transforming resistance and negativity.

Challenging Your Abilities

Whenever you act halfheartedly, you are missing an opportunity to take control of the energy of time. You are giving away your own power. The solution is to challenge yourself. By taking on challenges, you draw the power of time to you. By including what was excluded, you gain energy and knowledge. You can begin by noticing what needs to be done, and then do it. For example, if a job has been priced on the basis of materials and time, you could experiment with ways to do it faster and use fewer materials, all without jeopardizing quality. If you are in sales, you could take the initiative to contact clients in order to find new ways they can benefit from your services.

You can also exercise your abilities by acquiring new skills. Try to learn something new every day. It does not need to be a major thing. It may be the unfolding of a small talent or extending yourself slightly more than you are accustomed to. At the end of the day record what skills you have learned. Writing them down helps to draw the experience into the body.

On an inner level you can challenge yourself by learning to observe and by asking questions. For example, you can become aware of your posture, the way you speak, or the quality of your thoughts. Can you improve any of these? When you feel restless, see what happens if you ignore the urge to move about and sit through it instead. You can challenge yourself to listen better, to give others a little more space, or just to breathe more gently and evenly.

Look for the answers to questions that are relevant in any situation: Can I be more focused? Can I participate more? Remind yourself that there are levels of participation, and that there is no reason to settle for less than full involvement. If you are honest with yourself, you must admit that it is always possible to give more. Ask yourself: Why not take on the challenge of participation? Challenging your abilities is like being in a healthy competitive relationship with yourself.

A company can challenge its abilities in the same way, through keen observation and sincere questions. What needs attention? How can we make improvements? How can we streamline the flow of production? How can we sharpen quality control and guarantee timely delivery? The more precise the questions, the clearer the course of action will be, and the easier to dedicate energy to it. Instead of feeling at the mercy of circumstances, you will regain control and sharpen the competitive edge.

Developing your abilities will be most effective when you also challenge your assumptions, your weaknesses, and the parts of yourself or your business that seem to be dormant. These are the areas where the most time is lost, so here lies great potential to get control of time. Our assumptions keep us small while our weaknesses are usually nothing but unexplored areas. The reluctance and fear that may arise when you approach such an area are signs that you are entering 'forbidden' or unfamiliar territory. To challenge your abilities is a way of becoming at ease with the unknown, and of making the hidden power of time your own.

Overcoming Obstacles

Facing an obstacle is like encountering a roadblock; you are about to lose time and the connection with your goal. Overcoming the obstacle swiftly lets you continue on your way, regaining control of time.

Obstacles are often the result of change, which means that overcoming obstacles is a never-ending practice. It is better to face an obstacle sooner than later, to prevent it from growing and spreading into the future. Even a small obstruction invariably points to something that needs attention, to a problem at risk of growing.

There is no way of knowing in advance when an obstacle will show up, or how much damage it will do, but there are early warning signs that a problem is about to emerge. If you encounter difficulties at the outset, they will almost certainly intensify with time. For example, when we received messy art work from a client, we knew that during the production process problems would keep piling up. The likely result was that we would have difficulties in meeting our goal of delivering quality on time. Even getting paid might be a problem.

As soon as you have a sense of losing control, you need to tighten the reins promptly. Instead of letting problems dominate the work flow, you or your team can take charge. Look into time, into the future; let your awareness merge with time. Then you will find yourself doing the right thing.

You can prepare for obstacles by extending your awareness to embrace the entire flow of the project or the whole company. By letting awareness expand in space, like opening a protective umbrella, you create sensitivity to potential problems. There are fewer surprises. For example, I would sometimes practice holding in my awareness all the space from the front door of our building to delivery and shipping at the rear, and then expand to cover the entire sales region, as if it were in the same space. Gradually, a more global awareness emerged. Similarly, when we received an order for a job, we would imagine the entire production process, from the moment of receiving the job specifications until the delivery of the finished product, and even the receipt of payment. If your awareness spans time and space, fewer things will go wrong. More intuition seems to be available, and you have the means to pursue fresh opportunities.

When you control time, you can reserve the 'best' time and the best you have to offer for growth. As you learn to overcome obstacles, you gain confidence that your actions will produce results. You develop the faith that out of a positive action a positive result will sooner or later emerge. When your actions bring positive change, you become convinced that it is possible to draw out the best in each situation. Relying on your willingness and guts, you discover that in a way, the path to success is simply one of overcoming obstacles.

Transforming Resistance and Negativity

Resistance and negativity poison the atmosphere and interrupt the flow of work, resulting in a waste of time. Until you face them, it is impossible to control time.

Resistance and negativity seem to have their origin early in life. As children we try to conform to expectations and cultural patterns, becoming more and more isolated from our deeper feelings and thoughts. Resistance expresses the gap between who you are supposed to be and who you really are. Negativity comes when you are unfamiliar with your own vitality, reflecting resistance to action. Over time resistance becomes a habit. It makes you feel paralyzed, 'freezing' time.

Resistance sets in when you refuse to cooperate or participate in a particular situation. Internally you go on hold, waiting for things to be over. You tell yourself you wish you were somewhere else, doing other things. Since you cannot imagine anything positive happening, you hope things will go away or change by themselves. You 'park' your consciousness or focus on judging others, without being willing to look at your own lack of participation. In time, resistance grows into indifference, a sense that 'nothing is happening'.

Once you notice resistance and negativity arising, it is best to address them quickly. Dare to face the situation. There is no need for a strategy other than staying with it. Be present and available. Since resistance halts the activity, the key to counteract it is to start doing again. Action will reactivate the flow of the work, the flow of your energy, and the flow of your time. Find a way to participate in what is going on around you, and you will be taking control of time.

Resistance and negativity are allergic to willingness and enthusiasm, the natural by-products of being in time. If you manage to muster up these good friends, they will quickly uproot the patterns of resistance. At first, this may seem forced. Your resistance and resentment seem overwhelmingly real. But negative thoughts actually come to mind for no other reason than that they have done so many times before. They feel utterly familiar, like the clothes you wear, but they are not the real you. The pattern of negativity was established in the distant past; it is artificial. If you do not change it, it will keep recurring, but when you approach the job, the project, the day, even the moment with willingness and enthusiasm, such patterns will stop arising.

A simple exercise to deal with resistance and negativity is to do a small, simple task ; you might clean your desk or write a letter. Remember, resistance indicates you are holding back, and it is necessary to take action in order to get the energy flowing again.

Another approach that may elicit fuller participation is to ask some simple questions of yourself or your co-workers: How can I help? What works? How would I like to do this job?

Whatever you do, do not give up. Remember your commitments and refresh them. Remind yourself of past results, and apply the lessons you have learned: Continue to work and get results; focus on time instead of on yourself.

Occasionally, your negativity may be directed towards a particular person. If you maintain your focus on that person, repeating the same thoughts over and over, the negativity will only increase. Performing a task that requires cooperation may melt this attitude— now you are both in the same boat. If you can bring yourself to listen to what the other person thinks and feels, open communication will bridge the gap between you. As you find ways to communicate, your negativity will dissolve and eventually you will rejoin the flow of time.

When you are having difficulties with a particular person, you can also imagine being that person—being in his shoes, having his responsibilities, seeing through his eyes, and living his life. A wider perspective will bring a feeling of caring and diminish the sense of separation. Negativity will ebb away, and you can begin to appreciate what this person has accomplished and the obstacles he has overcome. This practice also creates a sense of joy in the accomplishments of others, which helps you link to time's dynamic.

Resistance and negativity leave residues in the body that impede work's dynamic flow, just as pipes full of sediment hinder the flow of water. How can we prevent negative memories from sowing seeds of resistance and even aversion? How can their roots be eradicated?

It helps to generate 'positive time', positive feelings, thoughts, and actions that plant the seeds for a positive future. Positive feelings, healthy thoughts, and a light and caring atmosphere reactivate the flow of vitality, gradually replacing the seeds of negativity and eradicating the roots of resistance. For example, you can recall times when you worked well, alone or with others. Or you may imagine beautiful situations and successful projects. The body and mind are ready to respond to positive energy.

> **Waking up to time** is knowing what you do with your time.
>
> **Taking control of time** is timing when you do what with your time.
>
> **Mastering time** is refining how you do what and when with your time.

Begin by imagining a positive situation or result. Gradually shift from the thoughts and images to focus on the feelings they generate. Creative visualizations, enjoyable memories, and thoughts of positive accomplishments all activate the flow of feeling throughout the body. Can you imagine adding a glow to these feelings, letting them radiate through the body and beyond? In this way it is possible to recreate the energetic foundation of body and mind and prepare a fertile soil for sowing seeds of success and joy.

Mastering the Energy of Time

When surfing in the ocean, timing is crucial. If you are behind time, the wave you are trying to catch will disappear; if you get ahead of the crest, it will crush you. Controlling time is like riding the crest of a wave, using its power. Mastering the energy of time is like a surfer mastering the energy of the sea.

What you experience as the pressure of time is simply time's energy. It can work either for or against you.

When you are behind time and wish to catch up, or when you are ahead of time, anxious about the future, you perceive time as an external force, working against you. But once you understand how to take control, time will not pressure you. Its energy will help the mind become clear.

You can learn to master time's energy when you have to meet a deadline. A deadline has a meaning in time. It links the present moment with a specific point in the future. It demands that you work wholeheartedly. The deadline dissolves the partition between the present and the future, and this is precisely what is so helpful, because the energy of time is no longer divided. The energy of time flows freely.

Being aware that you cannot afford to waste any time, you channel the energy of time directly into action instead of first thinking about it. Your concentration links your awareness directly to the energy of time; they merge, like two rivers coming together. At first, your awareness spans the time between now and the deadline. As you embrace time this way, your awareness deepens and extends further into time, before now and beyond the deadline. Increasingly time feeds back new insights on how to proceed. You begin to embody the power and intelligence of time.

We often had this experience. For example, on the morning after the 1989 Loma Prieta earthquake, the business world came to a momentary standstill. One of our clients, Wells Fargo Bank, needed an urgent announcement for its 20,000 employees. We printed, folded, and distributed the leaflet the same day. On another occasion, Autodesk, a software manufacturer, ordered 65,000 sixteen-page booklets on Friday afternoon at 5:15 PM, for delivery Monday at noon. We had just enough time that afternoon to pick up the necessary paper, and instantly all cylinders were working at full power. No time or energy were wasted; we were totally engaged. Time's energy became real aliveness.

Deadlines are one way to test your mastery of time, but whenever you quicken your energy and link it with time, you are beginning to master the energy of time. You are able to promote the positive and change or transform the negative. One way to do this is to learn to 'cut' time. For example, sometimes we would estimate a job to take seven hours of press time. Then we would ask: Can we do it in six and still maintain the same standards of quality? You can cut time by setting your own deadlines. This leads to a respect for the potential of time. Searching for more time becomes like mining for precious gems.

Another way to master time is to 'expand' it. This involves developing greater awareness—not only of specific moments of time, but of the moment between moments. For example, normally you are aware of leaving your house in the morning; the next thing you know, you are sitting at your desk in the office. The hundreds of moments in between have gone by with very little awareness.

Time's negative pressure originates in these gaps of awareness. When you are not aware, time shows up by surprise, catching you off-guard. But if you can link your awareness to each moment, and even to the moments between moments, there are fewer gaps in time, and you find an abundance of time. When you expand time in this way, you capture the energy and the knowledge contained in each minute moment.

Can you make the moments when you are unaware smaller and smaller? The more you can do this, the more your being and time merge. Then your energy is automatically charged by the energy of time. Your mind opens, receiving all the knowledge contained in time. You feel more intuitive, because less knowledge is excluded. As your awareness comes 'in' time, fewer problems arise, and there are no errors to set straight. This is what it means to be in time.

Every situation has a positive and a negative side. The negativity shows up as heaviness, suffering, and conflicts. The positive side is light, open, and dynamic. Time controls which side manifests. Mastering the energy of time from moment to moment, you make things lighter, and direct your own destiny.

Mastering Time

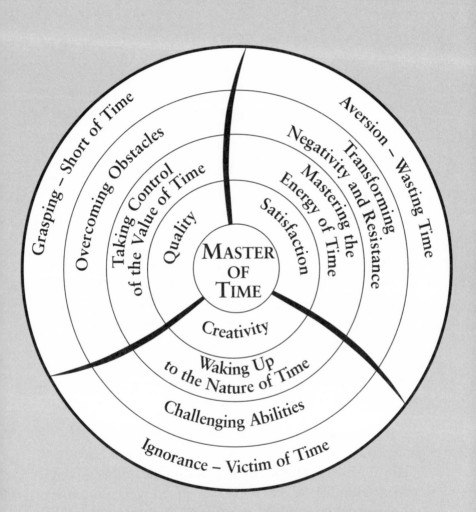

6

Instant Success

When we learn to truly cooperate,
there is no limit to what we can accomplish,
and to how deeply we can enjoy our lives.

When you work, the best you have to offer are your body and mind and the ability to express their unity. Your well-being and success depend upon how harmoniously each functions and integrates with the other. Whatever you do and whatever you say express the body-mind as a whole. When your actions and words are spurred on by the vitality of time, the activity of working vitalizes your being.

Body and mind are both equally important. When you are sick or old and dying, your limitations become painfully clear. The mind may be lucid, but what can you accomplish if the body can no longer function? And even when you have abundant energy and the willingness to do whatever is demanded, you are not necessarily effective and productive. You may lack a compass that keeps you headed in the right direction.

The way body and mind are used determines what you learn in life, what contributions you can make, and how much you experience in wisdom and love. When body and mind work together harmoniously, life has meaning. You are in touch with the spirit of being alive, with your heart as your witness.

Activating the Spirit

Without a body or a form, the spirit cannot manifest. An organization needs people, a location, an actual plan, and a product, and the workers must have a desk or workspace they can call their own. Yet without a mind, the form is empty. You may be willing, and resources may be available, but without a vision, a goal, or the ability to use your creative imagination, you will drift. Body and mind together, fueled by the breath, bring you to life.

Body, breath, and mind: These are the three gates to spirituality. Just as with human beings, the spirit of the company is determined by the health and integration of the mind with its body, against the background of time—the breath of life. Opening these three gates will activate the spirit of both the individual and the company. An organization needs to keep an eye on the overall spirit, and always be intent on improving it. Both employees and managers need to integrate and transform their realization of what makes up the body and mind of the company and how these elements relate to time. This is what it takes to remain on the cutting edge and be successful on the long run.

Body

Individual	*Organization*
Physical body	Workspace
Physical nourishment	Equipment (safety, use)
What you do with time	Productivity
Satisfaction (when working with the body)	Results (when getting things done)
Applying oneself	**Cooperation**
Transform negativity	Everybody acts like an owner

Breath or Speech

Individual	*Organization*
Breath, speech	Workflow
Vitality	Consistency
Being in time	Opportunities do not last
Joy from working well	Efficiency
Anxiety, worry (uneven breath)	Instability (unreliable performance)
Personal deadline set standards and goals	Working with deadlines 1- 3- 5-year plans
Bringing thoughts and feelings together into action	**Communication,** bringing people together

Overcome obstacles	Reduce waste
	Mind
Individual	*Organization*
Aspirations	Goals
Attitudes	Plans
How you work	How to conduct business
Skills, strengths	Specialty and niche
Weaknesses (laziness)	Shortcomings (complacency)

Everything has its own body, breath, and mind, even a product or service. Take a bottle of wine: The bottle is the body, the flowing of the wine is the breath, and the taste is the essence of the wine—the mind. The bottle, in turn, has its own body, breath, and mind: its actual shape, its easiness to handle, and the quality of its design. Each single part has this tripartite structure—even the wine itself may be said to have 'body'. The same is true for printed text, hardware and software, the meal in a restaurant—everything!

Similarly, this principle applies to all elements or segments of a company. For instance, to be complete and effective, promotional material always needs to express these three elements. By summarizing the essence of the product or the service in three single

97

words or one sentence, the image of the company is enhanced.

Body, Breath, Mind

The spirit of the individual or a company comes to life to the extent that these three gates are open, active, and integrated. And the opposite is also true: Emotionality in the individual or recurring problems at the company reflect a malfunctioning in body, breath, or mind. Since the gates are intimately connected, the underdevelopment or overactivity of one always affects the other two.

When your energy is held back or stuck, for instance, you become uncertain. You may lapse into laziness, which leads eventually to depression and even despair. On the job this will begin to show up in results. Your work lags behind; you lose orders and fail to meet deadlines. Selling becomes unnecessarily hard, production is frustrating, and cashflow dives into the red. When this slump takes place on the level of the organization, the company begins to lose its grip.

What is the root of these problems? In the model of body, breath, and mind the diagnosis is simple: One of the three gates is not open or not working properly. Resources are underutilized, the results or benefits remain unclear, and aliveness is missing. When such symptoms manifest, it is time to draw out the power and clarity of body and mind, and to integrate their energy and knowledge. For they determine the growth and success of all endeavors.

Communication, Cooperation, Responsibility

Many means are available to activate, integrate, and transform body and mind, directing them towards increasingly higher levels of productivity, efficiency, and benefit. The most immediate, direct applications involve improving communication, expanding cooperation, and deepening responsibility. Every potential difficulty, each conflict in any situation (on a global level even the threat of war) will immediately turn toward the positive when people are dedicated to better communication, more cooperation, and accepting responsibility. Activating any of them will instantly improve overall awareness and results. Skillful Means refers to the cultivation of cooperation, communication, and responsibility as the 'Instant Success Approach'.

Through cooperation you show your willingness to put your body to work. Taking responsibility displays commitment and the enthusiasm to take on challenges and to respond to what is happening. And like the breath, which feeds body and mind with vitality, it is your speech or communication that expresses the unity of body and mind.

Together communication, cooperation, and responsibility determine the soul of the company. An improvement in any of them immediately promotes the well-being of both the individual participants and the company as a whole. By fully cooperating you contribute to making the whole greater than the sum of its parts. This process can be ignited or sustained by communication. Success depends on the responsibility you are prepared to take. Reliable cooperation, essential communication, and wholehearted responsibility enable you and the company to go beyond assumed limitations.

To improve communication, cooperation, and responsibility, split the participants into three groups. One team focuses on communication, the second on cooperation, and the third on responsibility. At the beginning this may be a little chaotic, but it will make for lively exchanges as you discuss your experiences at the end of the day or week. Since each quality affects and includes the other two, the results will have three-fold power. Eventually, working with communication, cooperation, and responsibility becomes like singing in a choir. Each individual takes a specific part in the extended melody, while keeping in mind the harmony of the whole.

The Instant Success Approach is about learning to care. When you communicate, cooperate, and respond with care, the team you work with will function as one mind, one energy, and one heart. The effects will ripple throughout the company, reducing spoilage, increasing productivity and efficiency, and establishing a sense of fulfillment for all involved.

Communication

Every aspect of your presence conveys something about your life. There are many different forms of communication; not just speech, but gesture, glance, silence, facial expressions, and actions—even omissions. You move in a sea of communications.

Communication is the lifeline between people. Without communication, individuals become unnecessarily isolated, undermining themselves and choking off the growth of the business. When you suppress your insights and intuition, for example, or assume that others already know, or do not want to know, a basic disconnection occurs. Communication heals this separation, bringing together what was apart or divided.

What, When, and How

Good communication has a *what*, a *when*, and a *how*. Communicate what is helpful, in a timely and inspiring way. Then the result can only be positive and joyful.

When you intend to work at your communication, start small, nibbling away at the behaviors you wish to change. Listening better and interrupting less often will already make a difference. Trying to be a little more clear, a bit more caring, a little less self-protective will open up the lines of communication. Since your work situation gives immediate feedback on your progress, you will have a sound motivation for persevering.

It is important to learn *how* you usually communicate, by steady observation. The mind has to become aware of itself. This will take time, and when the habit of observation takes root, you may not like what you see. You may even be discouraged by the content and the extent of your communications, as well as by the way you communicate. But if you continue to observe, the reactions that shape your communication will gradually become less automatic. Learning to observe seems to make more time and space available, providing you with more opportunities to respond differently.

Start by questioning yourself. Do you tend to interrupt when someone is talking to you? Do you look people in the eye? Are you listening with interest, or are you just thinking about your next response? Is your mind drifting off? These habits are not hard to notice, and soon the habit of awareness itself will become a pattern. Over and over you will realize, "I am doing it again." Even though nothing seems to have changed, the openness and confidence needed to bring about change now emerge.

Communicating Self-Image

Too little communication is harmful because it limits possibilities. Too much can be a problem as well, making it difficult to identify what is essential. In both cases, there is often a self-image in the way.

If your communication is excessive, take a deep breath once in a while, or take a break. Give other people some time and space. Let them speak their mind. Ask yourself *why* you like to communicate irrelevant details. Are you communicating with care for what the other person needs to know? Or are you simply keen on projecting something about your self-image—how you wish you were, how you fear you are, or how you would like the world to see you? For example, giving the client a lengthy explanation of why a job is late and what went wrong, is not only unnecessary, but a way of passing the blame on to someone else. Can you let go of fear of blame and shift your concern to communicating clearly and directly?

Care to Communicate

Communication is all about caring. As Tarthang Tulku points out, *If we do not care enough to communicate well, all we can truly communicate is our lack of caring.* If you really care about whether the other person understands, and about your working together, you will naturally make an effort to communicate honestly, concisely, and clearly. In contrast, if you do not care, you may say one thing but in fact communicate something else altogether. The message you are transmitting is not just in what you say, but also in *how* you say it. On many different levels, you are signaling the real intentions behind your words.

Caring can be cultivated, but it takes time. If you start to practice caring, in the beginning you may only be able to pretend. Still, your wanting to care is itself a kind of caring. If you persevere in expressing care, the patterns of indifference will begin to shift. Caring has a momentum of its own, and over time it will develop naturally.

At work communication needs to concern the work itself: An organization depends on the continuing flow of information. At our printing company the docket or job order was essential communication. We made sure that the docket contained every bit of information related to a job at each stage of production. Caring meant making the docket accurate and complete, so that the job could flow smoothly from prepress to delivery, setting the stage for repeat business. In other companies it might be the flow of office memos and e-mail, correspondence, or financial records that is central. But in any company, making sure that the people who need to know are kept optimally and promptly informed is a key to both smooth productivity and a relaxed workplace. The wish to care can lead you there.

Honest Communication

In clear communication there can be no playing games, no gossiping or creating divisiveness—honesty is required. Honest communication means putting forward your plans, admitting your weaknesses, and bringing up difficulties. There is no benefit in hiding, or in covering up mistakes, or in holding back from asking for help.

It is possible to practice honest communication on your own, but it is easier with the support of a group, and the impact goes deeper. The group functions as a witness, strengthening each member's resolve. The group might be your company's senior management team, or several people working together on a specific project, or any group that interacts regularly.

Honest communication does not imply saying everything that is on your mind. It is not about displaying your personality, but about improving the character and performance of the company. Its purpose is to make each individual's knowledge available, drawing out what is important for the company. The main focus is always to look for solutions. It helps to inquire: "What is going on?" "Why did you do it that way?" "How can we make it work?" Asking questions creates space for knowledge to come forth.

Facts Only

The quickest way to improve communication is to concentrate on communicating facts only. Business communication is for the purpose of finding solutions and making decisions. When everyone sticks to the bare facts, much confusion and unnecessary inner dialogues can be avoided. For example, in a production meeting, the salesperson does not need to communicate why a scheduled job has not arrived in the shop—only that it is not there, and when it can be expected. Irrelevant details weigh the meeting down. Of course, if the reason for delay is that the client is in the hospital, that is a fact to mention and act upon.

'Facts-only' communication needs to be frequent enough to make sure everyone knows what he or she needs to know, but not so often as to become a waste of time. The same applies to meetings; their duration is to be set in advance, and they should begin and end on time. And every meeting should lead to a decision, even if the 'meeting' is no more than a casual conversation about a particular aspect of a job. The exchange of information should never end with someone left dangling, unable to proceed because a decision is still up in the air. Nor should communication end while

---

Musts for Meetings

- Well-prepared agenda distributed in advance (include reports)
- Determine length of meeting
- Start on time
- No reading during meeting
- No unscheduled breaks
- No walking out
- No personal, emotional issues or statements
- Find solutions
- Make improvements
- Make decisions
- End on time

---

there is still some ambiguity, even on a detail. That uncertainty will be sure to follow the job. Also, do not bring your personal agenda or old grievances: It is not a meeting of self-images.

It is tempting to break the 'facts-only' rule. But whatever the reason for breaking the rule—excuses, resistance and negativity on the one hand, or overexcitement and elation on the other—the result invariably is to interrupt the flow of work. The mind stops, and energy is drained. In that same moment positive action is on hold, and an extra effort will be required to start up again. In contrast, emphasizing facts only and aiming for helpful solutions penetrate resistance by making sure everyone remains connected to the flow of work.

If done at the appropriate time, 'chatting' about this and that, with no immediate business at hand, can also be a way of communicating care. Asking a colleague about the children shows that you are interested. This kind of exchange can provide a healthy basis for facts-only communication at other times. Communicating facts only clears the mind and keeps the channels of decision-making open. What needs to be done comes to light easily, and the knowledge required to do it is readily available. Friendly communicating of facts only releases all kinds of blockages, allowing for more openness—a fertile soil for cooperation.

Listening to the Inner Voice

Much of communication takes place within, in the form of inner dialogue. This form of communication—which often consists of relentless rehashing of past events or projections of the future—is usually not productive. Yet there is a form of inner dialogue that has great value, although it is frequently ignored. This is the inner voice, which communicates what the body and mind know.

The inner voice should not be confused with the whisper of insecurities and worries. It reflects a deep kind of knowing or intuition. Look for it in the slight reaction that occurs when you repeat your own limiting assumptions, such as "I guess it will be all right . . . ."

The inner voice will express itself in different ways, depending on the job you are doing. A machine operator who is about to make a mistake might later report a moment of unease, so fleeting that it was easily ignored. For a salesperson calling on a client, there might be a brief discomfort, a sense of pushing the client too hard, or of ignoring an opportunity to make a sale. Developing awareness of this subtle inner voice can prevent having to reprint a job or losing a sale. It can mean the difference between failure and success.

Communicating with Your Environment

Everything around you is alive, and participates in a mutually supportive interaction with everything else. Everybody and everything is an equal partner with the rest of existence. You influence the environment, and it in turn 'informs' you of what is happening. Like the cycle of breath, taking in and giving out, this interaction nurtures and sustains life. The senses too function in two directions, inwardly and outwardly; they are the windows of communication between your body and mind and the body and mind of your surroundings.

People who work with machinery can expand their sensitivity to the equipment, not only to maintain it, but also to run it properly. Through the noise it makes, the vibrations it produces, and the smooth working of its parts, the machinery actually 'tells' the operator how to run it properly. In our organization, we urged each pressman to treat the press, the paper, the ink, rags, chemicals, and especially the job docket as equal partners in the production process. Once the pressman became sensitive to the qualities of paper, the paper 'communicated' how it should be treated, and how it was affected by the temperature—whether it was too cold or too damp for printing, or dry enough to cut and fold.

This kind of comprehensive knowledge is available all around you. You can find out for yourself what makes up your environment, and how it communicates. Your pen, your computer, memos you receive, the delivery truck, other people—and you yourself, of course—should be treated as equal partners. Be open to them and respond to their needs. Together you do the job. The more open and receptive you are, the more knowledge is available for making good decisions.

Cooperation

When people cooperate, their bodies and minds literally join forces. The personal is transcended. Working well together melts divisiveness, as separation yields to unity. Cooperating is like weaving a fabric: The threads interconnect evenly, and the colors match harmoniously. Cooperation guarantees that operations run smoothly, without any gaps or breaks. When cooperation is wholehearted, everyone experiences the sense of flow that is inseparable from joy.

Cooperation improves by acknowledging whom you depend upon and who depends on you. Listen to your own needs as well as those of others, and do not be afraid to voice them. By helping each other when you have a chance, by reciprocating and dividing up the work, you create the cooperation that becomes a reliable force for success.

Playful Cooperation

On the job and in daily life, the main obstacle to cooperation is believing that your own feelings and opinions are more important than anyone else's. The problem is, everybody thinks this way! People will fight for their opinions, and would actually rather hurt each other rather than look for a common ground. Good cooperation is based on the opposite; 'personal' likes and dislikes yield to the common goals, allowing you and your co-workers to find each other in a new way.

How can you create such a bond? In general by putting the vision and benefits of the work or the urgency of time at the center. When a conflict arises, do not stop to analyze differences and to defend positions. Instead, emphasize the urgency of time and your mutual connection at the level of finding solutions. Encourage everyone to advance whatever ideas and suggestions might help the situation, while keeping the focus on getting the job done.

This process is like two hands reaching out to touch one another: If everyone stretches just a little bit, each person can join hands and work together. Once the connection has been made, energy will flow more freely. Knowledge can be exchanged without hesitation. Doing things right and—most of all—doing them together becomes the norm.

It helps to approach the practice of cooperation playfully. When there is a task nobody is keen on doing, you may want to offer to take it on. Exclaim that you are the one who wanted to do it first! In our case, a new supply of paper might be needed at 5:30 PM to keep the presses running. Rush hour is not a desirable time to go across town to a paper merchant. Volunteering in an exaggerated but good-hearted way takes some of the tension off the issue and makes working together more lighthearted. Others may immediately offer to help you in return.

Urgent Cooperation

Every business has clear deadlines. Whether we like it or not, working consists of meeting one deadline after another. Deadlines can have a stimulating effect, establishing cooperation naturally and quickly, and bringing out the best in everyone.

We once had to produce an overnight newsletter for a Hewlett Packard Users Group convention. The newsletter was scheduled to appear for four consecutive days. Each day around 2 PM the text would start to arrive in bits and pieces, but the last articles would not come in until 7 PM. The challenge was to print 6,000 copies of this full-color, forty-eight-page newsletter and deliver it to six different hotels by 6 AM the following morning. We rose to the challenge, working together, cooperating perfectly without any lapses in awareness. It was as if the job did itself. Together we were able to accept the pressure and take advantage of it, and to experience the joy of working together well.

Friendly Accommodation

Most people are immersed in their own thoughts. Instead of turning both inward and outward in the way of Skillful Means, they turn mostly inward. They do not seem to care about anything apart from their direct personal concerns. Nothing could be more damaging for a business. On-the-job caring is critical for safety, or to avoid duplication, and also to complement and balance the members of the organization. A lack of caring about the results of a project immediately endangers the potential of cooperation. Quality falls off, the client is dissatisfied, and the workers lose an opportunity for being content with their work.

Practicing cooperation makes 'friendly accommodation' to others the norm. Each person's energy and knowledge become part of a positive cycle of productivity and personal inspiration. If you want to practice in this way, it is important to become aware of the subtle ways in which people undermine each other. So often someone at a meeting will bring up an idea, only to hear, "Oh, we tried that. It didn't work." This response aborts the idea before there was a chance to examine it. Yet behind this suggestion another idea might be hiding. It is more positive to expand and build on another person's creativity, and in the process, stimulate everyone's creativity.

Responsibility

Responsibility may not be a popular subject with most people. You are busy enough as it is; another load on your shoulders is the last thing you need. You are forever receiving new jobs and tasks, and are wary of taking on another responsibility. It seems smarter to conserve your energy and protect your time! But renouncing responsibility makes you a prisoner of your work. You wait anxiously for the end of the day or for the time when you can quit altogether. Deferring to those 'in charge', you feel resentful. By refusing responsibility you leave your power at the door.

Taking responsibility turns this destructive pattern around. It implies not merely accepting whatever comes your way, but exercising your total ability to respond—your freedom to act. It is your mind in action, and in taking responsibility you express your level of compassion.

Leadership

Over the years we tried every management style imaginable. In the beginning the organization was centralized like a wheel held together by its hub. Next, we completely decentralized, with department heads supervising the flow of work and the subdepartment heads coordinating personnel issues. We tried weekly meetings with everyone attending, and meetings attended by department heads only. There were get-togethers with 'whoever is responsible for a particular problem' or 'whoever will be responsible for meeting a certain deadline'. For years, we had neither typical middle managers nor hierarchical lines of supervision. Gradually we began developing team management.

If you want to develop a management style that encourages more responsibility or leadership, you may have to go through a similar period of experimentation. It can be a long ordeal, but eventually, through trial and error, you will arrive at a truly democratic approach. It becomes evident that no one job or responsibility is more important than the next. Running the shipping department is as vital as accounting, or sales, or production management. Everyone is equally responsible for getting the job done well and on time. The key is taking responsibility, with everyone responsible for all that needs doing. This does not mean that you have to do it all or be involved in everything, but simply that you cannot afford to ignore anything. All of us are in the same boat together.

If you are in a management position, be sure not to consider the workers fixed resources. In addition to providing them ample opportunities to acquire skills and external techniques, emphasize the cultivation of inner resources. External training and internal development go hand in hand, developing inner confidence, self-motivation, independent thinking, and the ability to cooperate. Skillful Means workers will start to act as though they were the owners of the company.

One effective method is to give each staff member more than one area of responsibility. The advantages are multiple—individuals have new opportunities and different challenges, and eventually get a grip on the working of the entire organization. For example, in our case one of the press operators not only did print jobs, but also supervised a spoilage reporting system and was responsible for purchasing ink. Having multiple responsibilities and being willing to do whatever it takes helped everyone become more flexible. The drawback was that some responsibilities ended up on the back burner. But that just meant we had to make an extra effort to refresh our commitments; otherwise, they would have soon been forgotten.

Being responsible for paying bills on time may be the quickest method to elicit responsibility. You have to plan, coordinate, and constantly make sure that money keeps flowing. You learn to integrate time and money. When the flow slows down or turns off, supplies stop, employees become anxious and leave, customer loyalty is at risk, and you cannot support what you set out to do. Although you may suffer sleepless nights, being responsible for money provides a great opportunity to inspire, organize, and ensure achievements.

What Are My Responsibilities?

Every job has its own responsibilities. When they are defined too broadly, they will tend to overlap with other people's responsibilities, preparing the way for conflict. If your awareness is not well enough trained to take in the entire range of your responsibilities, there will be room for problems to take root. On the other hand, if your duties are defined too narrowly, you may become blind to anything else, and simply hide behind the excuse 'This is not my responsibility'.

Beginners whose responsibilities are not yet clearly defined can practice by asking, "How can I help?" Of course now and then anyone should come back to this basic question. For beginners and key personnel alike, it is important to extend responsibilities into time, making weekly schedules, as well as schedules for six and twelve months.

Here is another practice: Make a list of three things for which you are not responsible, and compare it with lists made by others. One of the women working at our company presented her list in a class, saying she was not responsible for cleaning the men's bathroom. At first everyone agreed, until someone pointed out that when visitors left the press, the last place they passed before reaching the lobby was the men's bathroom. If there was an unpleasant odor, that would be their final impression of the company. Taking responsibility in this case did not mean that she had to clean the bathroom personally, only that the dirty bathroom could not be ignored.

Responsibility depends on awareness of what needs to be done. Avoiding responsibility on the job may be a sign that something needs attention: Your awareness may not be sufficiently developed or integrated with the awareness of others. Somehow or somewhere you may have ignored knowledge available to you and given up on your ability to respond to a situation.

By tracing the omission, you can find out what this knowledge and energy represent.and release the emotionality that it holds. More importantly, you discover some knowledge that has been overlooked. It may not be easy to follow up on what you know, but your ability to respond is beckoning to you. When you are willing to be responsible, you can afford to listen to seemingly negative thoughts and discover what they have to tell you. If you find yourself thinking, "I will not respond to this situation," you might as well declare, "I settle for being less alive."

Mistakes

You can invite responsibility by owning up to your own mistakes. When you make a mistake, watch to see if you try to find reasons and excuses why something went wrong. Do you blame someone else, or even yourself, as though providing an explanation for the failure was the end of it?

To see through this defensive attitude, you can practice saying, "I take full responsibility for my mistake." But watch out: Saying and doing are not the same. Taking full responsibility also means correcting the mistake. In the business world responsibility usually revolves around time and money. If you do not make a gesture towards the financial or material consequences of your mistake, you are not responding fully. Cleaning up your mistakes stimulates you to grow and improves the atmosphere within the company. Perhaps you are incapable of making a financial gesture when a mistake has cost the company money, but you can certainly sacrifice some of your time to restore what has gone wrong.

The most effective way to take responsibility is to commit to deepening your level of concentration and caring, so that fewer mistakes occur in the future. Look for dullness and heaviness as indicators that you have not taken full responsibility at this level in the past, or that you are shying away from it now. Taking on small duties may help you to start up again. Offer your help; clean up that mess—do it now!

Responsibility for Mind

To develop responsibility, we need mindfulness, the knowledge of how things actually are. This means being aware: Aware of our actions and thoughts, aware of their effects on others, and even aware of their consequences on a global level. This awareness allows us to always respond appropriately.

—Tarthang Tulku, *Skillful Means*

Developing mindfulness begins with learning what goes on in your mind while you work. As you become more aware, you wake up to the qualities of your experience. There are several benefits. You are less likely to forget things and more likely to take on responsibility. You begin to understand that there is no need to let yourself be subjected to whatever comes to mind; you can actually choose what to place there. This makes your plans for action more reliable.

Strengthening mindfulness will activate your intention to take responsibility for your work, since the results you achieve are a reflection of your mind. Discovering how the mind works enables you to improve the way it works, thus sharpening your results. The results give you feedback on what else needs to be improved and how to go about doing that. This cycle of positive feedback stimulates personal growth and strengthens the business.

Responding Positively to Challenges

As mindfulness develops, you become a witness of your own responses from moment to moment. The instant of responding is critical, as it sets the stage for what follows. Usually the mind dictates the mood, and the mood dictates the response. But you can learn to encourage yourself to respond positively right off the bat. The best time to practice this is when challenges occur.

At such times there is a tendency to feel overwhelmed, to resist or even try to ignore the challenge, or perhaps to respond automatically. But if you make a conscious effort to respond positively to challenges, you take the power of the present into your own hands.

Generating positive intentions may feel false or phony at first; your impulsive negative reaction, having become a habit over the years, may appear more real than this new response. The unwillingness you feel may simply indicate that in the past you repeatedly renounced responsibility in one way or another. Now you are hitting the walls of lethargy you built to protect yourself. Yet the mind is open; nothing is fixed. Taking responsibility is your response to being alive, and a demonstration of loyalty to what you value.

Acting Like an Owner

If the tellers in a bank or the sales staff in a store would act like owners, the bank and the store would probably thrive. Customers would love doing business there, for they would sense that the staff showed a genuine interest in their needs. The atmosphere would be refreshing, since working this way is more fun. In short, everyone would benefit, on both sides of the counter.

To develop such a mentality, it is vital to notice even the most fleeting feeling of dislike toward your work, your business, your boss, or yourself for what you are doing. Such momentary aversion provides you with an alibi for not participating. Unless you own up to your experience, things will get worse. If you can get hold of the deprecating thought, you will not yield to the mood that encourages you to renounce responsibility. You can make an effort to rekindle your vision, and to create a structure for the best way of working on your own and with others. As you reclaim your own life and revamp your ways of doing business, a love for discipline will ignite spontaneously.

You can put a stop to passivity and discover how to improve your job and get the results you want. Ask yourself what new duties—or old ones, swept under the carpet a long time ago—you would like to take on. Take ownership of the work you do and the way you do it. Take satisfaction in knowing you can be counted on to do what is necessary, do it as best you can, and finish on time—not just today or tomorrow, but on a continuing basis. Consider every part of the company your business. In acting like an owner you can become a leader. When everyone demonstrates leadership, everyone participates equally and wholly.

Working Well Together

By practicing communication, cooperation, and responsibility you assemble all the ingredients necessary for Instant Success. Developing one of these factors includes the other two. For example, in cooperating you need to open communication horizontally and vertically, within yourself and with others. Cooperation requires willingness and enthusiasm for learning, as well as taking responsibility through working wholeheartedly.

Communication, cooperation, and responsibility each have three doors that open into optimal effort, creativity, and result.

Let us take cooperation as an example, since that is probably the most enjoyable and effective way to get results and work well together. The three doors of cooperation are:

- Communication of Cooperation
- Cooperation of Cooperation
- Responsibility of Cooperation

The overview in the chart on the following page gives you ways to see how communication, cooperation, and responsibility each play a role in cooperating.

In the same way, responsibility and communication each contain the other two. No matter where and how you start, each one leads to healthy, harmonious, and productive ways of working together well. Instant success is guaranteed.

Three Doors to Cooperation

Communication of Cooperation	*Cooperation of Cooperation*	*Responsibility of Cooperation*
Speech	Body	Mind
One's own unique value	Unique value of others	Appreciation for the whole
Looking outward	Being open	Caring
Delights	Appreciation	Benefits
Sharing knowledge	Encouraging others	Succeeding as a group
Common bond	Unique values of each member	Integration
Trust	Focusing on the positive	Overarching concern
Growth	Vitality	Productivity
Relying on each other	Helping each other	Caring
Making decisions	Finding solutions	Overcoming obstacles
Encouraging	Positive	Supportive
Mutual understanding	Mutual respect	Creative inspiration
Joining forces	Joining energies	Joining ideas
Decline in conflicts	Decline in obstacles	Decline in mistakes
Work flows	Work flows evenly	Work flows consistently
Joy	Satisfaction	Success

7

Positive Knowledge

Viewing freedom as intrinsic to our being, we discover that our lives are what we make them. All options are open, our choices unlimited. When we have knowledge, time presents us with infinite possibilities for change.

At any moment you can decide to change what you are thinking or doing. As a human being you have the choice to place positive thoughts in the mind, and avoid adding to your own suffering or the suffering of others. Exercising this freedom wisely depends on becoming aware of positive and negative attitudes and actions, and discerning their effects on your own body and mind, on the organization you work for, and the environment in which you live. Developing such positive knowledge and putting it into practice is a critical aspect of Skillful Means training.

Positive action opens what was closed, calms down what was overactive, and integrates what has grown apart. Drawing out the best, it stimulates creativity and wholeness. It enlivens experience and lets you take advantage of opportunities. On a personal level, choosing the positive joins together thinking, feeling, and acting. On an organizational level, aiming for the positive connects the vision of the company with the daily activities of each employee. The company becomes increasingly unified and integrated through time: an ongoing vision in action.

Positive knowledge marks the beginning of success. At our company we practiced three ways to develop positive knowledge: cultivating appreciation, guarding against negativity, and strengthening the positive.

Appreciation

After my first week at Dharma Enterprises, Tarthang Tulku asked me how we were doing. I started to list the various problems we were encountering. He gently interrupted me: "Always start with appreciation: Appreciate your opportunities." This teaching became the guiding principle of my daily life.

Based on recognition of the preciousness of human existence, appreciation is a springboard to positive knowledge. You may not realize the power of appreciation until you give it a real try. For a few weeks, set out to appreciate the opportunities that work offers you. A good way to start is to list them. Work provides you with a living, and may grant a sense of camaraderie. It probably also offers a host of opportunities for acquiring skills, being creative, getting results, and learning about yourself and others.

Appreciation extends not only to what you get out of working, but also to how you work—the activity of working itself. Here lies the greatest potential for positive change. Developing the art of working ignites the spirit of being alive. How you work expresses your appreciation for life and for the fact that you can work. Work allows your contributions to count, and directs your mission in life. In experimenting with how you work and observing the results, you refine your inner resources, your mind, and most of all your ability to care. The art of working becomes a vehicle for change. Each job, each gesture you perform becomes a work of art.

Obstacles to Appreciation

For all its power, appreciation may at times be difficult to sustain, especially when you feel guilty or find yourself blaming others. Guilt and blame close off the space for appreciation, blocking positive knowledge. They may be indicators that you have blindly followed models established by others. By becoming dependent on others' judgments, you may have diminished your own sense of value and integrity. The mind tightens, preventing dynamic engagement in life. Appreciation reverses this dynamic, opening the mind to respect and warmth. Ignited by appreciation, guilt and blame can be transformed into a desire to act constructively.

The main obstacle to feeling appreciation may be that we simply do not recognize the unique occasion of being human. We are not accustomed to being grateful for what we consider to be our birthright. And only rarely does education remind us that we can develop the mind and grow as human beings; that in fact this may be our main task in life. Not realizing our opportunities, we may find little to appreciate.

Cultivating Appreciation

One effective exercise to stir up appreciation involves repeating over and over, silently: "How happy I am to be here, how happy I am to be here." It may sound silly, but try it for yourself. For a while we greeted each other in the morning in the same way: "How happy I am to see you!" It does wonders. Another exercise is to stand up straight, open the eyes wide, and smile from ear to ear. These exercises are energizing, especially when you find yourself working half-heartedly.

Do not be misled by the simplicity of these exercises. Exaggerating helps. It loosens things up. Telling each other jokingly how happy we were, we would burst out laughing. In the beginning, acknowledging appreciation does feel phony, because you are not really feeling appreciative. Remind yourself that negativity is just as unreal. Go ahead and pretend: One state of mind is no more real than the next.

These exercises are not about the truth; they are about breaking through to more openness and a different view. It may take just a slight shift in awareness to switch from darkness to light, from a closed mind to openness, and from apathy to care. Appreciation offers that possibility. It massages the mind, restoring its natural openness.

Guarding Against Negativity

Becoming aware of the power of negativity may impress you just as much as realizing the value of appreciation. Negativity contracts, darkens, and inhibits life's vitality. It limits the possibilities that life offers.

Although awareness of negativity points the way toward positive change, it is habitual to resist feeling your own negativity. Negativity is pervasive and ingrained, and it is disheartening to notice so many negative forces in and around you. It is like diagnosing a serious illness that requires medication. Unaware of it, you may feel negativity as a kind of uneasiness that leads you to look outside yourself for distractions and approval.

You may also close your eyes to negativity by telling yourself that your moods, actions, and prospects are determined by circumstances; that fate is responsible for your failures and successes. But just the opposite is true: Your basic nature is open and you have the power to change. Acknowledging what is negative enables you to take charge of yourself. You begin to develop knowledge of the positive. As you learn how to improve your attitudes, you rekindle your vitality. You create the conditions that will let you fulfill your destiny.

Here are five ways to guard against negativity: learning to observe destructive patterns, challenging weaknesses, becoming familiar with the power of confessing, discovering the possibility of massaging time, and detecting low levels of awareness.

127

Destructive Patterns

Although you might wish, and even demand, that everybody around you be positive, a more realistic approach to positive knowledge is to start by recognizing your own negativity. Every thought, every gesture or action seems to have a tinge of negativity to it. It may be just the tiniest trace, hardly noticeable, but treacherous nonetheless. How easy it is to believe in the content of negative thinking, and to accept that it reflects at least some part of the truth! At our company, we regularly practiced observing our own thoughts and speech, and gradually we made a shocking discovery— we were both the agents and the victims of a vast conspiracy. Negativity was the ringleader, but its co-conspirators were everywhere, both inside the company and outside. For all this time we had unknowingly been encouraging each other to believe our own negativity, and to accept that of others.

Negativity seems to be in the skin, the eyes, the blood. This is a humbling realization, especially since it continues on its own accord. In theory you are capable of doing something about it, but in practice, the mind has been programmed to negativity for so long that you are no longer aware of it. You accept it as the way things are and feel no urgency to change. People who do experience urgency, in the face of death for instance, have been able to make drastic changes in their lives.

What are the antidotes to negativity? How can you use the mind's power in more positive ways? One strong antidote to negativity is to practice acting the way you wish to be. Ask yourself: "How would I like to be? How would I like the company to be?" Perhaps you dream of being less angry, more cheerful, more up-beat; you may envision the company being more dynamic, the employees more caring.

Visualize this changed reality. How would you walk, talk, and act if you were this brave, honest, or responsible person? The more details you can think of, the better. If you act on what you imagine, you will become it, more and more. Making these changes for the positive are not intended to soothe or beef up the self-image, although they will help you feel better about yourself. Rather, they contribute to making you, your organization, the economy, and the environment more wholesome. Simultaneously they instill in you and your co-workers more dignity, integrity, and creativity.

Challenging Weaknesses

Work mirrors your strengths and weaknesses—it is impossible to hide from the results you achieve. On the job, negative patterns and feelings are reflected in low-quality output or downright mistakes. If you can resist the temptation to find excuses for yourself or to disclaim responsibility, you will notice that mistakes provide you with valuable feedback. A mistake is like a signal. It draws attention to a negative pattern that stands in the way of quality, timeliness, and satisfaction.

Once you have identified a weakness, you can challenge yourself by taking on the responsibility to strengthen it. The same principles underlying your strengths can be applied to your weaknesses. If you are not sure how to perform a particular task, first analyze one that you know well. For example, you may be skilled in meticulous handwork. At our company employees responsible for fulfillment for a large order had to have this skill. Often such a person would think of this skill as a limit, saying, "I am only good at this; I cannot do sales." But exactly the same skills that let you perform collating, handling, packaging, and shipping a large order apply to doing sales. A good salesperson needs to care about the client, the in-house communication, and in general about follow up and follow through.

Suppose you are the handworker, and now you have to do sales. Since you may not be accustomed to communicating smoothly and succinctly, you may be convinced, "I lack the skills for this." But when you challenge your weakness by applying your strength, the client will be delighted by your high standards of care and your focus on detail. The only switch required is to bring the dexterity of the hands to the mouth.

To benefit from your mistakes and work on your weaknesses, you will have to watch for the pitfall of renouncing responsibility. If you keep your commitments vague and refuse to participate fully, you are shying away from the chance to reveal your weaknesses. Eventually this holding back leads to feelings of resistance and resentment.

You can treat these feelings the same way you handle mistakes—as clues to hidden weaknesses. Can you trace them back to a point in time when you deferred or refused responsibility? You can make this into an exercise by reflecting on your workday. Suppose that on reflection you feel some resentment about a meeting. Tracing it back, you may realize that early in the meeting a decision was made against your better judgment. Instead of expressing your opinion or proposing an alternative, you held back. Since you let the opportunity to participate go by, you are left with a sense of incompleteness. If you let this feeling pass too, without taking some kind of action, resistance and resentment take firm root.

Power of Confessing

Many people hesitate to make changes, believing they must know in advance what the changes will entail, and what they themselves will become in the end. They fail to realize that transformation is an unfolding process and that strategies for guaranteeing the perfect outcome are useless. In the process of changing, your entire perspective alters, and so do your possibilities. All you need is resolve. Tell yourself you want to change and dare to take the risk.

You can strengthen the resolve to change by acknowledging a weakness, mistake, or negative pattern, saying to yourself, "I will not make this mistake again;" "I will not repeat that behavior again;" "I will take care of that." Avoid saying, "I will try . . . ." Trying is simply not good enough and using the word may subtly undermine your confidence. Watch out especially for one negative pattern that is the father of them all: 'confessing' your negative patterns while at the same time justifying them as minor or inevitable. "Oh sure, I know I'm a quitter. I've always been that way. After all, I'm only human." This false confession keeps the negative patterns firmly in place, leading to a dead end.

Confessing your mistakes to yourself with sincere regret can diminish negativity. Take the time at the end of the day to review what you have done. Confess your mistakes, and decide not to do them again. The regret has to be genuine, or confessing is just an empty gesture. Occasionally, acknowledge a mistake to others. The resolve to change toward the positive is strengthened by having witnesses, though not judges.

Massaging Time

It is not too late to heal the past and release the blockages produced by negativity, for the effects are still with you. This involves looking back on the past, using creative imagination. In your mind you can ask yourself, "How could I have responded differently?" It does not matter whether it would actually have been possible or not. Creative imagination loosens up the mind and melts residues of the past into more openness.

A related exercise called 'Massaging Time' can be done at the end of a project, or better still, at the end of the day. Start by recalling and reliving the day from the beginning. Look for tension. For example, if you became upset at 11 A.M. and feel a surge of emotions as you review that situation, stop there. Go back in your mind to a time well before the onset of that particular event. Slowly start forward again, paying attention to the details along the way. Describe to yourself exactly what was going on, as well as the setting in which it took place. When you reach the point of emotionality, you will probably find that at that moment the rest of experience vanished; 'being upset' usurped all your energy.

By reliving the moment, you can bring back those ignored details. Focus your attention on everything else around you at the time—the location, the furniture, the colors, other people, the time. In recalling as many particulars as you can, you are restoring the fullness of that moment. Your negative emotions no longer stand out and have the power to take over.

If in practicing this exercise you do not succeed in defusing the negative feelings right away, return to the beginning of the day and repeat the process. Do this as often as necessary, loosening your specific focus. As you create a more expansive space, the blockage—a moment frozen in time—will begin to melt. The sensation of tension melting may be vivid. It is as if you are recapturing the energy of that particular moment.

By going back and forth in time, eventually you will not even be able to contact the emotion. It is gone. You have removed the negative residues. The corridor of time is open again, and your energy flows smoothly. With practice you will be surprised how easily you can dissolve emotionality. When the anger or fear you identified with has disappeared, you may actually feel somewhat at a loss. But this turns out to be a very positive state, for you are more free.

On occasion, you might try extending this exercise back through your whole life. You may discover emotionally-laden periods where time became stuck. These past negativities are still capable of blocking you today, making life needlessly heavy. By massaging time, however, the blockages will start to open up, leaving you feeling light and joyful.

This way of healing the past can also benefit the other people who were part of old conflicts and emotional situations. Even if they are not with you any more, the entanglements may persist, calling out to be healed. Once you have opened the period of time, you can instill it with positive thoughts and feelings, even adding an overall glow to it. By replacing negative time with positive time, you activate the power of what is positive.

Low Levels of Awareness

Negativity comes in all shapes and forms. Ultimately, negativity is a sign of a low level of awareness. For instance, making up reasons and excuses for not doing a better job, or drifting down to the minimal and accepting 'this is how it is' are sure signs that awareness is dull and that you are caught in some negativity. By sharpening awareness, you can counter this tendency to settle for less.

Learning to recognize signs of low awareness lets you set an alarm, a reminder that negativity is active. When you find it hard to focus, accept superficial answers, or give in to a routine, this inner alarm goes off. Probably the most obvious indicator of all is confusion, which may signal in turn small-mindedness or a lack of planning. Painful as it may be to recognize these pointers, if you let them motivate you, real change is possible. With heightened awareness, freedom and the positive qualities within are restored..

Strengthening the Positive

Unless you are willing to acknowledge the dark and heavy side, your positive intention will be fleeting, undermining you and your decision to change. But if your focus remains only on the negative, you may be overwhelmed by persistent frustration. Therefore, it is vital to strengthen the positive at the same time. In this way the process of developing positive knowledge becomes more playful, while the effect remains just as healing; it is like taking a double dose of medicine.

Several ways to reinforce the positive are: learning from history, acquiring new skills, creating a positive atmosphere, giving 'five percent more', evaluating results, developing discipline, and cultivating humility.

Historical Truths

Knowing the history of the company or business and being aware of the efforts that were involved in making it what it is today sets the stage for a positive future. When you appreciate the successes and failures of the past, what worked and what did not—and why—you are ready to build on what is positive.

In any business both old-timers and people who enter a new situation are often tempted to start from scratch. This is especially likely if the old regime leaves in a hurry and does not take the time to share their experience. Newcomers like to believe that they know a shortcut to success; that they can do better. This attitude inevitably leads to rounds of duplication, wasting time and energy and preventing the intimacy that comes from sharing knowledge.

In our case, we experienced problems in both directions—cases when knowledge was not duly passed on, and examples where valuable experience was not received with an open mind. We learned the hard way that the refusal to tap into the available information is painful and costly. As we learned from our mistakes, we began to remember our own history as a matter of course. Trainees were asked to take notes as a part of their apprenticeship and a way to preserve knowledge, and outgoing employees were given time to write the necessary manuals and train their replacements. The aim was to make it seem as if there had hardly been a transition at all.

A sensible adage in business is "If it ain't broke, don't fix it." Yet it is equally important to recognize and let go of patterns of failure, and to refresh the commitment to the vision that guides the enterprise. Certainly the desire to improve prevents routine from setting in. Determined to get good results, you can build on the positive accomplishments of the past with new enthusiasm, vigor, and discipline.

The sense of personal history works in the same way at a more subtle level. Again the idea is to focus on what worked and what did not. To strengthen the positive, it helps to remind yourself of your own accomplishments and the achievements of others. Listing what has been done and sharing these lists will generate a shared sense of joy and enable you to tap into your own vitality, using it for change and achievement.

New Skills

Acquiring new skills provides a natural basis for confidence and integrity. Each new level of mastery will reaffirm your faith in yourself and your ability to get the results your actions aim for. Try to learn something new every day—a technical skill, a mind skill, people skills, a skill at applying yourself, anything at all. Through learning you grow. What would you like to learn? Merely by showing interest and keeping it up, you will find out what it takes, and before you know it, you will be on your way to becoming a specialist. But do not stop there—pass on your knowledge to others. Encourage them to develop their talents too. Everyone needs to move on to new responsibilities.

Positive Atmosphere

The mind and heart are receptive to beauty and warmth. They have the power to activate our dormant capacities. There are many ways to bring this about. Cheerfulness and kind words are helpful, though flattery and excessive praise are not. It is rewarding to beautify the surroundings: The senses thrive on cleanliness, colors, order, and beauty. At our facility we made improvements almost daily as we tried to follow the idea of making each place we left more attractive than it had been when we found it.

One approach is to clean up, paint, decorate; in short, make the setting more conducive for working. Another is to imagine your work area in its ideal state, and then bring that quality to the fore. If you can recognize it in the mind, it can come into being. Through imagination, you begin to reform your surroundings.

Five Percent More

One of the most exciting Skillful Means exercises to strengthen the positive is to remind yourself that you are always capable of giving five percent more. In our company, we posted large banners reminding us: "5% More!" These banners did not mean we should work more hours, but simply that we could give five percent more than we were automatically inclined to, in every dimension. First five percent more energy, then another five percent, then five percent more focus, and so on. It became obvious we had not been running on all cylinders; we were simply coasting, satisfied with surviving. We had been happy with a six on a scale of one to ten, and that meant our energy always tended to drift to lower levels of intensity.

To our surprise, once we did give five percent more energy, we were less tired and eager to do more. It was at once embarrassing and illuminating to see that giving five percent more could actually become normal.

If you practice this way you will reach a pinnacle where increased focus and energy meet—the summit of the positive. But who knows? Maybe there is another five percent beyond that!

Evaluating Results

To evaluate results, all you need to do, both individually and as a group, is to take a few minutes at the end of the day to look back at what has been accomplished. Feel the satisfaction of the results of that day. When you feel good about your efforts, a special sensation flows through the body. You feel like saying, "I had a good day today." Try to contact this feeling or sensation regularly. It forms the basis for strengthening the positive in the long haul.

Discipline

Discipline is often considered heavy and constricting—something to be avoided at all costs. You may believe that discipline will prevent you from being spontaneous. But discipline is not just a method for making yourself do unpleasant things. On the contrary: It takes discipline to set aside time for what you value, for what nourishes and inspires you. Through discipline, you become a disciple of what you think is important.

Without discipline no one can do a job well; results are bound to be haphazard and flawed. With discipline, you bind all the forces and resources necessary to achieve your goals. Living with discipline lifts the burden of disorder and discontent, and frees you to be engaged, flexible, and creative.

To be a positive factor, discipline must stem from inner knowledge, from what you know is right. In choosing a discipline for yourself, you show your care. Developing discipline—not too much and not too little—requires articulating your targets and standards, evaluating your plans, and assessing your situation. What kind of atmosphere suits the work best? What structure fits the bill? Initially, discipline is likely to work like this, resulting in structures and guidelines. After a while this framework may shift, or even fall away. Ultimately discipline is not rigid—it is alive and supports aliveness.

At the heart of all discipline stands knowledge of time, since it is in time that inner knowledge emerges. If you do not appreciate time, it is difficult to appreciate discipline. By the end of this day, your life will have diminished by one day. Does that realization make you want to organize yourself for tomorrow, and for the rest of your life?

If you are aware of time—if you know the nature, the value, and the energy of time—you will use your time well. Each job is like a lifetime: You need to make a good start, do it right and enjoy it, and be satisfied at the end. No matter how great time's pressure, try to stay in touch with the cycles of each undertaking, with the beginning, the middle, and the end. With discipline you bring order to your life, time flows smoothly, and all goes well.

Humility

Humility comes from recognizing that your knowledge is incomplete. There is a certain power in acknowledging that there is something you do not know, and in being ready to learn what knowledge you need to acquire. At least you know you do not know, and this has always been considered the beginning of wisdom. From a business point of view, acknowledging that you lack a certain expertise or are unsure how to proceed invites others to share their knowledge with you. Shared knowledge accumulates, enabling everyone to act more appropriately.

Humility restores openness, honesty, and freshness. It dissolves the contrast between the negative and the positive, so that you can embrace both aspects in each experience. Accepting the wholeness of each situation supports and directs you in asking an essential question: What is important? Humility leads you back to appreciating the opportunities and possibilities that working offers. Then negative and positive do not matter so much.

8

Inner Resources

*Work is a mirror of awareness, and the quality of
our awareness sets the tone for how we work.*

Sometimes we are satisfied with the work we do. We
feel creative, energetic, and simply have a good
time. We welcome challenges as they come along, and
at the end of the day we are content with what we have
achieved. Then, without warning, everything seems to
change. Every single task presents an insurmountable
obstacle, and we find ourselves dreaming of other times
and faraway places. The same work, the same setting,
and the same co-workers that seemed just fine yester-
day strike us as dreary and threatening today.

What is going on? Who is in charge here? According to Buddhist teachings, the mind is capable of creating both happiness and suffering. In the context of
Skillful Means, mind is our total response to being
alive. Can it be true that our own mind is responsible
for these inexplicable shifts, for our trials and tribula-
tions, our ups as well as our downs? To find out, and to

see what is possible in our work, we must get to know this mind.

This requires training in awareness. If you want to get to know and understand mind, consider your work a training ground, a school for human development. You and your work are teacher and test, and the results you get in working give you reliable feedback on the scope and strength of your mind. Your work speaks for itself, plain and simple. How you work is who you are. The results of your work carry your fingerprints—your personal signature of who you are and what you did with your time. Although the theory and practice of Skillful Means can help you, ultimately you are on your own. Now is the time to acquire self-knowledge and to be self-sufficient. You can make up your mind to do well. Simply say to yourself: "I will give it my best."

When you are working well, with concentration and awareness, you can observe suffering and joy in operation. You can challenge weaknesses and emotions as they arise and disappear again. In becoming aware, you are training yourself, and at the same time learning to take care of yourself at a deep level. The training takes place on the job—in the body and in the mind, while you work.

There is no doubt that you can strengthen the mind and that your actions can have more power and merit. You can set standards for yourself while you work, catch unproductive thoughts and laziness, acknowledge when something is wrong, and encourage yourself to take care of how you work. This awareness training makes clear that negative reactions such as dullness, guilt, and blame are strongly entrenched, and that to master them you need tools that will allow you to learn from mistakes and release the tension and disappointment that keep you from being more successful. As you learn to motivate yourself and see the results of the changes you make, you gain inner confidence, and your knowledge of the mind grows. You know that you yourself are the link between a vision, a plan, and the goals you aim for. By cultivating with care how you work, you will become a wiser person.

The only reliable means for discovering and training the mind in this way are the inner resources of awareness, concentration, and energy. If you think of sailing a ship, awareness is the captain, concentration the boat, and energy the wind. Together they determine where to go, how to get there, and what it is like at your destination. Awareness surveys the options amidst all the distractions, while concentration focuses and channels your energy. These inner resources offer a chart of human potential and the blueprint for success. In business terms, they determine efficiency, productivity, and results. Together they determine what you accomplish.

Awareness

Awareness is like a light in a dark night. The stronger it shines, the better you can distinguish what is going on, inside you as well as outside. It is inseparable from being. When awareness is limited, your possibilities are restricted, and you tend to feel cramped, a prisoner of your own mind. With more awareness comes a sense of space, and your perspective grows wider. Lack of awareness manifests as suffering, emotionality, and the inability to realize targets and standards. As awareness increases, experience becomes richer. You begin to reclaim your authenticity and inborn ability to know what is right.

Awareness training is a fundamental practice in all Buddhist traditions. It underlies all the topics described in this book, and is the key to success in any of them. For example, focusing on the way you communicate and the way you use your time are awareness practices. To start working with awareness directly, however, takes awareness practice one step further. You are developing awareness of awareness, which ultimately leads to the mind directing itself.

The mind is accustomed to drifting off and being easily distracted. You may be sharply aware only in certain situations, as in emergencies or while taking an examination. Everyday awareness depends on bringing this same sense of urgency or determination to each situation, yet without straining or forcing awareness. Only when it is light and gentle can awareness ultimately sustain itself.

Awareness Training

Raising general awareness in a business will often produce substantial improvements. For example, one common problem in business is that the needs of the company and the needs of its employees seem to diverge, especially when it comes to time and money. The company needs projects done on time and within a budget. The workers may be more concerned with free time, while budgetary constraints have little meaning to them. How can the two be brought together?

If the conflict is identified and openly discussed in a way that invites everyone's participation, the awareness of the employees and management rises simultaneously. Almost immediately people start to work differently. As everybody becomes increasingly engaged, solutions tend to present themselves. If the initial division was about time and money, solutions will tend to arise from heightened awareness in these areas. As people become more sensitive to time, time's pressure diminishes. Feeling less pressured, employees may initiate innovations and desire to take on more responsibility, and the company will likely reward them for that.

Developing awareness builds motivation and restores the dignity of both people and the value of their work. At our company, we thought that inspiring ideas about awareness and responsibility would be enough. But this was a mistake. Specific procedures were also required, such as stricter guidelines and job descriptions. We worked with awareness by instituting checklists for printing and for outsourcing jobs. Bookkeeping was cleaned up until we could pass external audits without difficulty. Safety manuals and employee-benefits brochures were distributed. But still, we had trouble formulating clear lines of duty, and this caused conflicts and frustrations. At such times the struggle for success could seem harsh, an uphill journey. It became clear that we could not just cultivate awareness indirectly. Instead, we had to focus on a structured awareness training.

Eventually we learned to focus on developing awareness in three specific areas that equally apply to any business or organization: refining particulars, controlling waste, and countering confusion and forgetfulness. These areas or topics are crucial for increasing productivity, efficiency, profit, and the well-being of the workers. They can protect any organization from drifting downward and encourage employees to take on more leadership.

Refining Particulars
Anyone can refine an eye for detail. The details do not have to be special in themselves. A single sheet of paper on the press, the machine on which your livelihood depends, or a particular word in a text are both worthy of your undivided attention.

In refining the particulars of working, we learned that when we were upset or nervous, merely paying closer attention to some minor detail in the work space would automatically settle the mind and clear the head. A sense of well-being would replace any emotionality. It may seem paradoxical, but focusing introduces more space in the mind. Awareness deepens and extends, and more knowledge becomes accessible. This expanding awareness sharpened a sensitivity for needed improvements and created a buffer to anticipate possible obstacles and changes.

Particulars are important in any business, and especially in printing, which is a demanding, highly skilled craft. At all stages of the process overlooking a little thing can ruin a job. If there is a mistake in color, if the press is making marks on the paper, or if the printed work is handled before it is completely dry it will be necessary to reprint the job. To improve our eye for detail, we eventually decided to have at least two people look at every step in the production process. When one aspect of the job is particularly difficult, the rest of the job tends to be ignored. A second person may catch other faults.

We also emphasized that everybody can become more detail-oriented, not only in their specific task, but also when assisting others. When checking something before the actual print run, we often reminded each other that at least one thing had to be wrong. Could we spot this flaw?

The focus on details helped us improve our grip on the work. We wasted less time and made fewer mistakes. Beyond that, it was thrilling to discover that focusing on details somehow recharged us and fostered integration in the flow of work. We felt lighter and more engaged.

Controlling Waste

For our company the impetus for controlling waste came from the recession that hit California in the early 1990s. As our sales declined, it became second nature to watch for waste. We soon began to enjoy the practice. It seemed there was always some element of waste that could be eliminated. For instance, at that time we were spending $35,000 a year on messenger services. For less than that amount, we bought a small truck and hired a driver to do our own deliveries. We saved time, money, and much aggravation. Again, we established a guideline that for every job needing more than 5,000 sheets of paper we would get bids from three different suppliers. As soon as the paper companies realized we were bidding out our jobs, their prices dropped. Saving three dollars on every thousand sheets added up to a full-time salary by the end of a year.

To focus more attention on waste, we instituted regular spoilage meetings. Rather than blaming one person when materials were wasted, we traced back each step to identify what happened, and each of us made a resolve to avoid the mistake next time. Eventually, just recording spoilage numbers, without any follow-up, was sufficient to awaken awareness. For example, if time and materials on a job we had to reprint due to a mistake cost $2,000, and if we knew the profit margin on the next job in line was $200, then ten additional similar jobs would be needed to make up for the mistake. We reminded ourselves that in addition to time and money, spoilage has human and environmental implications. Thinking about all that waste had an immediate impact on everyone.

Countering Confusion and Forgetfulness

Awareness is an antidote to negativity, distraction, fear, and anxiety. It is also a guard against letting opportunities slip by. To cultivate this kind of awareness at our company, we would set personal goals, writing brief essays about what we wished to achieve. When our goals were clear, we would ask ourselves what opportunities the business offered to fulfill them, and whether we were acting on them. We kept in mind what was important to us while we worked, like athletes who think only of winning, nothing else. In this way we became less dreamy and more focused.

To further develop our awareness, at the start of each day we wrote down three particular things we wished to carry out or keep track of. For example, I might write, "Increase sales, meet payment deadlines, and be more sensitive to co-workers." This list provided a framework and became a resource that informed me whether I was on the right track. As I went through the day, I looked at it periodically to remind myself of my objectives. I found myself doing things that supported these goals without even realizing it.

The fact that we practiced Skillful Means as a group was an important stimulus. We would remind each other of a particular practice for that week, and we learned from discussing our experiences. Occasionally we made lists of individual and group accomplishments. We made schedules for what we committed to achieve in the next month, or in the upcoming six-month period.

All this helped us to remain focused on what really mattered and develop a steady awareness, but old patterns are well entrenched, and we still experienced many gaps in awareness. In our meetings we often spoke about our discouragement with our lack of focus. It was easy to become sad or angry at our own apathy. But we encouraged each other not to give up. Over time the training began to pierce through the patterns of not being involved. Commitment came to the foreground, and with it came aliveness.

As we developed more awareness as individuals and in the context of the group, we could sense a subtle, gentle transition from 'me' to 'us', from 'what can I get?' to 'how can I help?' and then to 'how can we do this together best?'

Concentration

Concentration gives awareness focus and holding power; it determines your level of engagement. Concentration connects the mind with gut-level energy, making it possible to take charge of the mind, instead of just accepting whatever comes up. As the bridge between awareness and energy, concentration integrates body and mind.

Concentration deepens through awareness of time. When you are aware of time, you naturally become increasingly involved in what you are doing—not behind or ahead of time, not too fast and not too slow. The result is that concentration becomes continuous and steady. As concentration links you to time, you can draw on the dynamic energy inherent in time. In practice you can set this sequence in motion by making a plan for each day, remembering your goals, and setting and meeting deadlines.

When much is at stake, or when emotions are involved, it is easy to remain engaged and concentrated. But when pressure is lacking, or if you do not specifically value what you are doing, concentration tends to fall to a lower level. At these times it is especially valuable to train concentration. Such training is not easy, for restlessness, strong likes or dislikes, manipulation, indifference, and watching for praise and blame all have a powerful effect on your ability to concentrate. They are like saboteurs, undermining what is positive. Yet their domination lasts only as long as you feed them with energy; they are not essentially real. If you persist with your training, concentration will gain momentum, and in time will become habitual.

Relaxation in Concentration

A good way to cultivate concentration at first is to squeeze your attention, firmly determined to hold your focus. Gradually concentration will become lighter. Good concentration is like continuous presence of mind. To make it steady, relaxation needs to be developed. When you are relaxed, thoughts become softer and less demanding. The feeling of internal relaxation will become the support for a stable focus, like a still pond on which the flower of concentration floats serenely.

A simple relaxation exercise at the beginning of the day takes no more than a few minutes, and gets you started with the right basis for concentration. Sit still, take a few deep breaths, and sense the breath as it comes in through both nose and mouth. This way of breathing will feed the vitality of the breath equally to the head and the torso. As you become aware of sensations on the surface of the body, or within it, you can enter into them, just as you would sink into the water in a full bathtub. Relaxing into sensations in this way expands into awareness of the entire body. It allows relaxation to spread throughout the body, and even beyond it. These feelings refresh and recharge you, and they will support your concentration. With relaxation, concentration becomes increasingly effortless. Steady involvement continues on its own accord, not needing further encouragement.

The focus of concentration will be different for different people. Whatever the focus is—making a profit, gaining a market share, or preparing an offering—it lies behind every single action. Concentration maintains the vision. When it is strong, everything you do contributes to realizing the goal.

Having a clear vision is like the traditional meditation practice of visualization. A meditator develops concentration by projecting a certain object, such as an inspirational image or a source of light. In the business world, vision and goals play a similar role. If the overarching vision slips out of mind, actions become more confused, and painfully familiar emotional patterns emerge. But if you keep the goal in view, emotions that confuse and muddle the mind will become more and more transparent, easy to penetrate. You can see for yourself that thoughts and emotions are like an overlay on clear awareness and the power it contains. As concentration deepens, restlessness yields to stable energy, and you experience inner joy, a natural byproduct of concentration.

Concentration culminates in full integration. On a personal level, body and mind are integrated, and your actions clearly express your vision. At a deeper level concentration will unify past, present, and future. Awareness extends in all directions, and you make the best of the opportunities time presents.

Energy

Energy is life's inherent vitality. You are already familiar with it: You breathe energy, your eyes show it, and your actions express it. All activity, even a thought, is a sign of this vitality. Energy is the force you need in order to give form to your ideas. When awareness is open and concentration high, it is possible to tap into and become energized by the vitality that you already embody. The breath and the senses are the gateways to this dynamic vitality. Becoming familiar with your energy is as important as developing awareness, for the level of energy you apply in your work determines the level of satisfaction.

If you are tired for no good reason, this is very likely a sign that your level of energy is low and needs attention. Feeling drained, you may automatically look for an 'emergency' to get your energy going again, but this sets in motion a vicious circle of wasting energy. Instead, it is of prime importance to find out when and where the leaking and draining of energy takes place and how it can be prevented.

Just like the breath, energy needs to go two ways: in and out. Any imbalance in giving and taking will cause unnecessary problems. If your energy flows mostly outward, you will become empty and burned out. Yet if you focus primarily on 'getting', without passing on what you receive, you will become anxious and ineffective. In the equal exchange of energy 'in' and 'out,' you display your natural vitality.

The feeling of burnout seems to be connected to giving too much without receiving an equal return. But can you ever give too much? After all, you can never give more than you have. Burnout may actually have a different dynamic, connected to not receiving enough. Somehow your expectations—of yourself and of others —are not being met. For instance, if what you receive at work consists primarily of a paycheck and some occasional praise or blame, you are not getting enough nourishment. In that case, the solution is to open and activate your relationship with other sources of energy. Since everything in life can activate your energy, this is not difficult to do.

The senses are two-way channels. This means that they can be the path through which new energy flows toward you. Sensing the world around you, you can receive energy from all that you see, hear, and feel. Without movement, 'touch' and let yourself 'be touched'. To practice this, try to imagine that objects are alive; that they can see you and can speak to you in their own language. If you allow the senses to interact with your surroundings in this way, they will feed back energy. In this dynamic exchange you find new vitality.

Of course, the same is true for people. Rather than emphasizing your goals and opinions when you interact with others, you can receive their ideas and ideals. Receiving this energy is facilitated by your asking questions, so that their creativity and caring have the opportunity to come forth. Their energy then feeds your own and recycles throughout the company, building on both your interests and commitments and theirs.

Inwardly, energy originates in the belly. If the heart is like a fire, and the throat gives the supply of oxygen, the belly or the guts provide the fuel that sustains the fire. But how can you nourish the belly? Most importantly, the breath needs to find its way there. If you suppress your feelings, or do not act on what you know you ought to do, the flow of breath to the belly will falter and eventually come to a halt. The mind may be willing, but you will find it harder and harder to do what you wish or what is called for. The antidote is to open the gates of your energy by breathing into the abdomen while imagining gut-level energy connecting with the head. At first emotions like resentment and negativity may come up, reflecting the way that life's vitality has been choked off. But if you continue to relax, and also do some physical activity, you will rekindle the flame of life that burns within you.

Levels of Awareness, Concentration, and Energy

When awareness, concentration, and energy are low, you tend to make mistakes and fall short of your goals.

You may start to believe it is your fate to be only sporadically successful. With limited access to your own resources, you will be incapable of feeling interest or appreciation, and tend to be scattered and full of doubts. Starting a new project will be difficult, and finishing it successfully will be even harder.

You can become aware of your own level of these vital resources by looking at the psychological patterns that manifest in the way you work. For example, low awareness brings confusion and the sense of being a victim of time. Anxiety, worry, and always feeling short of time indicate that concentration is erratic, keeping goals out of reach. With low energy, time is wasted; you miss the boat because of laziness or aversion.

There are two main approaches to counter flagging awareness, concentration, and energy. The first is to develop each resource individually: sharpen awareness, develop concentration, and learn how to use your energy. The second approach is to integrate all three at the same time, first taking them to medium levels, and then to high levels of functioning. Either way, refining your inner resources is the best way to develop your own potential and contribute to the success of the company you work for.

Developing Resources

If you want to work on awareness, concentration, and energy one at a time, begin by observing how each of them functions, what their tendencies are, and how to strengthen their operation. Just ask: "What is my level

of concentration?" Or "Right now, what is my level of
energy or awareness?" If you observe in a neutral way,
like an analyst looking through a microscope, your
question bypasses judgment. It is amazing how much
is revealed under your gaze; new worlds open. When
you increase awareness like this, it truly becomes an ally
and a teacher.

In becoming aware of your awareness, look for
signs of confusion or lack of direction. Notice whether
you are eager to make excuses. Is your work becoming
routine? This means that the level of awareness is low,
only partially functioning. Being conscious of time will
counter this problem. Asking questions can also help.
"What needs to be done? What is the overview and what
are the details? What am I ignoring?" Analysis brings
clarity back to the mind. Keep your focus on what is
important and what works.

Signs that your level of concentration is low include
feeling scattered, and producing inconsistent and
flawed results. The root problem is a lack of focus. A
restless and grasping mind, always on the lookout for
something else, will typically make you feel anxious
and rushed. Concentration improves by focusing on
the task at hand. Notice the restless fluttering of the
mind and gently bring your attention back to what you
are doing. Engage yourself again and again, a thousand times a day if necessary. Lead yourself back from
distracting thoughts and a grasping mind to a steady
focus. This way concentration will grow. Eventually it
will sustain itself.

When nothing makes you enthusiastic and keen, it is a sign that your energy is low. Energy seems to be inaccessible. You hold back and are resistant, unwilling to participate or to make commitments. You may actually tell yourself that passivity agrees with you, but even the smallest glimmer of greater awareness will make it obvious that opportunities are passing you by. You have become an outsider; you are left out, excluded from the action. Somehow the energy needs to get going again. The simplest way is to act. Instead of procrastinating, 'just do it now'. Do not even give yourself the time to ask why.

As soon as you start to counter confusion, anxiety, and resistance—malfunctions of the inner resources— you begin to experience more joy (through concentration), more satisfaction (through energy), and more meaning and appreciation (through awareness). Getting involved, acting, and then seeing the results of your efforts are stepping-stones to these positive qualities. Increased awareness restores openness, while concentration and energy bring back interest and inspiration. Together they restore the wholeness of experience and the beauty of working well.

Integrating Resources

The second method to counter weak awareness, concentration, and energy is to improve their levels simultaneously. To go from low levels to higher levels, it is best to learn skills or to focus on improving productivity. This will affect all three resources simultaneously.

159

At our company, we focused especially on productivity. Employees recorded their work activities, developing quantitative measures for what they had accomplished: how many units, activities per hour, per day, etc. Each of us registered the number of scans, rolls of film, proofs, plates, print and fold impressions, finished units, deliveries, sales calls, quotes, jobs in, purchases per department, and so on.

In addition to keeping track of the level of productivity at each stage of the job, we also posted the results. Initially, there was some grumbling about this, as some employees tended to compete with one another, and there was a certain suspicion of management. We offered no incentives for increasing productivity (this may have been a mistake), and imposed no penalties for not improving output (another mistake?).

As time went on, we learned that a small dose of competition among employees can actually be inspiring and productive, but that the most meaningful competition comes from competing with oneself. Once that lesson sank in, posting production figures prominently throughout the plant became an effective stimulus for everyone's level of awareness, concentration, and energy. Often, merely stating the facts is more effective than morale-boosting meetings. Facts are clean and impersonal; they are utterly convincing.

Increasing productivity emphasizes quantity and quality in time. Speed without spoilage calls on your capacity to care. Focusing on productivity not only gives better results, but also clears the mind, streamlines the flow of work or production, and reduces waste. In time this will lead to more enjoyment, more satisfaction, and fewer mistakes. More money and no complaints—everyone benefits!

In order to make further progress, and to sustain higher levels of awareness, concentration, and energy, you need to refine or quicken your energy. Working with the hands and the body on a strict time schedule will do just that. It is like building a new 'body of energy'.

Another way to refine energy is to do breathing and movement exercises that relax and revitalize you *while* you work. If you breathe lightly in the upper body and briefly hold the breath there, your energy will become lighter, more swift. Coordinating movements with your breathing will activate energy and stimulate a sense of presence.

There are also mental exercises that feed the source of energy. For instance, you can practice letting go of an opinion, or asking clear, unbiased questions of yourself and others. Energy also wakes up when you aim to make things lighter by finding solutions quickly, by being cheerful, and by demanding quality now.

Successful people seem to have endless supplies of energy. You can open the gates to this unlimited reservoir by being dedicated and lightly keeping your mind on results. Then concentration will link awareness and energy to time's vitality. This vitality is not located in the body, like a tank of gas in a car. Rather it enters the body through the breath, and through the interaction of the senses with the environment at large. Linking awareness to the breath and the senses, or to posture and movement, is another way to make this abundant energy accessible.

As you refine energy, awareness clears, releasing the stuckness of emotionality. Energy begins to move freely through the body, becoming brighter and more dynamic. Since you are no longer separate from the energy of time, you can control time and even master it.

Working with awareness, concentration, and energy for some time will convince you that low levels of these resources are not natural. They are just the result of bad habits, a kind of self-deception that can be unmasked. You can cure the disease of negativity, apathy, and indifference and regain your natural, positive qualities of clarity, inspiration, and vitality.

When you decide to tackle low awareness, concentration, and energy, you will automatically become aware of time. But you can also take the opposite approach. Awakening to time improves your inner resources. As you channel the power of time you activate your abilities, overcome obstacles, and transform resistance and negativity. Now time is your energy. This is the beginning of your ability to master time, using it to sustain creativity and successful actions. On the job this shows up in three ways: abundant energy, not missing opportunities, and no mistakes.

Awakening and integrating the inner resources often brings up a fascinating twist, a strange paradox. Even if you know that you are working better and feel happier, you are likely not to sustain this kind of inner work, but to fall back into old patterns. Why should this be? One reason is that you are accustomed to living halfheartedly. It has become a habit. The second reason is that when the inner resources come to life, you may become afraid. The increasing intensity of experience and the dynamic energy are new. Not only are you not familiar with them, but you rarely see examples around you. Fear of the lightness of being may direct you right back to the safe nest of mediocrity. At this level, working and practicing with others is important. It builds a steady base that gives you the inner confidence to pursue your mission of awakening potential.

ACE Interplay

It takes time to realize the open-ended potential of what you can achieve by cultivating the interplay of awareness, concentration, and energy (ACE) on a daily basis. The potential is unlimited. Developing presence of mind and skillfully using imagination and energy let you refine your working to achieve increasingly higher levels of creativity and accomplishment. New dimensions open up, and the mind begins to function at new levels. Awareness manifests energy and directs it into concentration. Concentration assures the work will be dynamic and alive.

Experience and the feedback it provides offer one way to learn, but it is just as important to study the concepts, the overview, the map. In our organization we never really attained the higher levels of achievement, yet working with the concepts was enough to lead us in the right direction. Learning the map of the inner resources by heart will expand the mind even when your experience does not keep pace. As the mind deepens and expands, your actions will gradually reflect your understanding. These two ways of learning, through experience and through theory, influence one another.

For each job, the interplay of ACE required is different. Sometimes a narrow focus and gentle energy is necessary; at other times a broader perspective or stronger energy is needed. Each work activity has its own texture, rhythm, and feel. The more you touch the feel of a particular job, the more you directly experience what you are doing. Such direct experience of working opens awareness, steadies concentration, and releases smooth, almost effortless energy. Working becomes an enjoyable, creative exchange of all forces at hand. Awareness brings in knowledge, concentration captures opportunities, and energy fuels progress —a cycle of positive accomplishments.

You do not need special instructions, guidance, or management techniques to use work this way. As Tarthang Tulku points out, awareness, concentration, and energy are like . . . *friends, guides, and protectors. These three resources allow us to awaken our creativity and intelligence. In this magical way of being, there is no limit to how much we can achieve.*

9

Questioning Mind

Questioning and being aware:
these are the most precious teachers. They dwell in the
heart of every human being who begins to awaken to
the waste and danger of an unexamined life.

Every situation, each problem presents us with a
myriad of possibilities for responding. But our patterns are strong, and we may not even be aware of having a choice. We simply think, "This is how it is." The
same problems seem to occur again and again. Often
we find ourselves drifting aimlessly, waiting for a crisis,
or hoping that things will somehow get better by themselves. What have we done with our power to change?

In a company, when a new person comes on board,
the fresh energy stimulates excitement. But when this
fades, we may sense discomfort, even fear that he will
rock the boat. Most of his suggestions have already been
tried anyway, and we know in advance they will not
work. His enthusiasm and insights receive only lip service. Even if we realize we have built a wall of defense,

we find solace and justification in having survived until now. We end up fighting for the status quo. But must we give our power away?

Perhaps we realize the company has lost its dynamism and urgently needs new direction, and hire an outside consultant to show us how and where to make improvements. A consultant brings in the ability to observe and ask questions, and analyse what needs to change. But do we really need someone else to tackle the tough questions or suggest the tough decisions while we hide behind their expertise? Can we not do this ourselves? All we need is an open mind and the willingness to change.

Anyone who has ever participated in a successful brainstorming session has witnessed at least some of the qualities of bringing an open mind to bear on a particular issue or situation. In such meetings you are encouraged to withhold judgment and build positively on the ideas that are presented by every single person. As new ideas accumulate, one on top of another, fresh points of view arise.

It is possible to take this process much further. Each of us has the capacity to stop in our tracks, observe what is going on, and ask the most basic questions: "What is happening? Why is it that way?" Analysis based on care, free from judgment, can revive the spirit of the company. When we start this inquiry, a glimmer of hope, a taste of new knowledge warms us to the task. Perhaps we do have the ability to know. This is the promise of knowledge that questioning can bring.

Promise of Knowledge

It is not easy to observe your own work or analyze a company strategy without feeling guilt or even shame. But you do not need to take these feelings at face value. They may indicate only that you are trapped, like a fish in a net. If you keep on pushing forward the net will tighten until there is no room to breathe. You can get out only by swimming backwards or turning around. Impatience and loss of temper are close at hand, but they need not stop you. Rather than telling yourself you 'should' relax, or that it is better simply to give up, start afresh. Reconnect with your inner strength—your ability to know.

If you look at a specific situation at work, what improvements would you like to make? What would make it better? When an answer comes, do not tell yourself you have tried that already; do not enumerate the reasons why it will not work. If you were the new employee or the outside consultant, what would your advice be? At this stage you may not really care that much anymore; you may have already given up. But you certainly cared when you started. Reconnect with your original inspiration when you took on this job.

Have you told others about your ideas? Have you listened to their suggestions and their aspirations? Maybe over time your co-workers have stopped talking with one another and have accepted the ways of working that everyone follows. But you can start all over again. If you had six months to improve your project or the specific ways of working in your department, what would you recommend? How would that affect others? Can you articulate your ideas and express the changes in numbers and dollars? If you ask questions and genuinely answer them, you begin to turn around the momentum of mediocrity.

For instance, rather than accepting how a client works and how your company responds, look for ways to improve the cooperation with the client in such a way that the customer benefits. What service can you offer that is needed and new? Instead of accepting automatic responses to such questions, pause for a moment. Observe, ask questions, and pursue creative answers. Even if things are going well, keeping a finger on the pulse of 'improvement' is essential to avoid decay and stimulate growth. Can you improve cooperation, production, and quality? Is the client really king? Do the people who work on the project concur on the best approach for the client and the company? If your approach is not fresh and wholehearted, the time and quality you give to a project may be inconsistent and marginal. Is the relationship with the client or the operation of the company gradually drifting towards lower levels of morale, service, and profit?

Questioning opens the door to success. Of course you need to apply energy and power to the new knowledge. But why would you not, once you really know what to do? Do you really need more people, better equipment, or additional money? Instead of resorting to a poverty mentality, start with the richness of new knowledge. Only then does it make sense to ask what else is needed.

Massaging the Mind

Learning to observe and ask questions is called 'Questioning Mind' in Skillful Means. It is probably the single most honest and effective way to make improvements. When you put it into practice, you will discover that you already have access to the knowledge of success. Maybe the sadness and frustration you feel at times are merely indicators that you are not acting on what you already know. Questioning Mind awakens knowledge, so that you can take action. The all-important first step is to know that you do not know.

When you apply Questioning Mind, do not expect a solution right away. When you stop and question, you are not even looking for the ultimate answer. Questioning Mind simply enables you to create more openness and to shine light on your inborn creativity. Can you discover what you are ignoring?

At the start it is a matter of massaging the mind, enabling fixed positions, responses, and habits to loosen. Ask yourself simple questions. Refuse to accept the same old answers. Continue thinking or talking where you usually tend to stop. You may feel bad about how indifferent people are, how unwilling they are to question, how closed to new insights. But negative judgments are only the dull veneer of knowledge. Rather than taking these labels at face value, you can penetrate to 'alive' knowledge—the ability to know. The honesty of your questions and the sincerity of your answers will expand your known into the unknown. You will discover that the unknown is yours too.

169

As long as you make assumptions or fail to examine beliefs, your world will continue to shrink. The smaller the range of options, the more fear there will be, and the more rigid your methods of working. But even here the light of knowledge shines through. You can trust the fear or resistance you feel as thresholds to imminent transitions. Once you start massaging the mind, encourage and motivate yourself to stay with your ability to observe and to answer your questions in a new way. This will give you access to new knowledge and restore within you the freshness of the newcomer and the wisdom of the outsider.

The possibility of change is facilitated by the truth of time—all things change. It is unnatural to try to keep things fixed and frozen. This is not about change for the sake of change, but about making use of the inherent nature of time, which provides the opportunity to change at any time. Right now your options are open: You can choose to be different. If you were promised a bonus for making any improvement in your own attitude, could you not do it? Just as the ocean produces one wave after another, each one always new, you too can be different in the very next moment.

How can you improve the service you offer or the product you sell? What other changes for the better can you make? How would you like the results of your work to be? These questions could stem from some kind of dissatisfaction, but they might also arise from the recognition that time presents again and again the opportunity for change.

Activating Knowledge

In order to achieve stability and success, your activities and progress must be based on the right knowledge. Competition—and ultimately survival—demands that you stand on your toes, look around, and aim higher. That is why it is so helpful to question your problems and challenge your limits. Questioning Mind leads you to the heart of the matter, recapturing knowledge that has been lost in the web of assumptions and prejudices.

Anyone can learn Questioning Mind. It can be an oral or a written practice. In the beginning it may be easiest to practice in a group. The more articulate the question, the shorter the route to new knowledge. Questions like "What were you thinking of?" or "Don't you understand?" tend to lead back into the familiar, the known. Questions such as "Why? How? What is important?" or "How else can it be done?" will usually be more effective.

Questioning Mind is a useful management tool for any organization or team. Initially there may be some resistance because people tend to support each other's assumed limitations; everyone puts so much energy into 'no change' that challenging limitations seems confrontational. But genuine questions show that you care about the company and the people who work there. Such questions have the power to neutralize and bypass hesitation and resistance.

Practicing Questioning Mind in a group requires a certain level of openness and trust. You cannot demand this of others, but if you feel the necessary openness is lacking, you can use Questioning Mind to investigate this problem by yourself. Try doing this in writing. By being honest and writing down creative answers to your questions, you will find your way through these obstacles on your own, particularly when you question your own skills in dealing with them. It may then be appropriate to address the issue openly within the group. Questioning Mind has likely created space in your mind, enabling you to see new options for moving beyond doubt and mistrust.

At times it is advisable to practice on your own. When you do this, it is best to write down both questions and answers, phrasing them as precisely as possible. In using a pen and paper, you actually give 'body' to insights that otherwise tend to vanish into thin air. Each written question is also an invitation to enter unexplored territory. When you do not know what to ask next, you can write "What do I need to know?" or "What would I like to know?"

Power of Knowledge

Watch to see if you fall into the trap of recycling old information. Ready-made answers are a disguise for justifications that have nothing new to tell. Giving reasons and excuses for problems and mistakes also do not help. At best they prove you did not do it on purpose, but that is self-understood, and furthermore, it is not the issue. Questioning that goes beyond these traps helps to open up the desire and the power to act differently. Ask yourself: "Could I have handled this problem any other way? How? Was there something I needed that I ignored? What prevented me from getting it? How would I suggest the same problem be handled in the future? How would I like to take care of it?"

Once you leave behind the usual answers to basic questions (often starting with, "I thought . . ."), fresh responses will come up, moving the mind into new dimensions. You will probably discover something unexpected. Perhaps somewhere along the line you have ignored a sign or excluded from the decision-making process relevant information that would have allowed you to respond differently.

The purpose in pursuing these different possibilities is not to make you feel guilty. Guilt is just another excuse. Rather, the aim is rekindling your ability to know. If you discover something new, something you have never told yourself before or heard before, your answer instantly brings aliveness. You realize how an unpleasant situation or poor result could be transformed. Since you found this out by yourself, you realize that nothing really limits you. You have the power to know. You discover the power of knowledge. You are free.

Questioning Mind should be an ongoing practice, in both good times and bad. Always keep a finger on the pulse of your satisfaction with your life, accomplishments, and prospects. This is as true in the business world as it is at home. For example, once the president of a large catering chain went on a three-day

Skillful Means retreat. The goal was to review his business strategy using only Questioning Mind. The first question was: "What are the current issues the company faces?" He framed the topics that came up into more questions: "How can the managers of forty-five restaurants take on more leadership? Should he hire a general manager to enable him to continue expanding into other business opportunities? Should the head office be moved to a new and growing area? What needs attention first?"

During the two-hour Questioning Mind sessions, he analyzed the familiar obstacles in new ways, and soon he noticed a general feeling of heaviness dissolving. As he entered the unknown, he had to face moments of uncertainty, but out of these new clarity emerged. Simple answers to complex situations arose as the energy of body and mind were refreshed. Emerging from the retreat, he dispatched a string of new plans through e-mail messages to the head office, setting out goals and courses of action, each reflecting his own insights and deeper aspirations.

Obstacles to Questioning Mind

When the mind becomes aware of new information and points of view you have never before accessed, you feel uplifted, as if something inside is smiling. This feeling may show up in the moment just before some specific new understanding emerges, as you relax into the activity of knowing. But sometimes, before this inner relief appears, you may become restless, irritated, or tired. When you are new to Questioning Mind, you may think that resistance, restlessness, and fear are signs that you are not doing it right, and you may want to stop. But what is really happening is that you have hit a wall—you have reached the limits of a dogma or conceptual understanding. This may indicate you are at the gate of new knowledge. If you have the courage to persevere and stay with the process, questioning and giving the best answers you can, opening will come.

Fear is a form of resistance that comes up before entering the unknown, as the inevitable consequence of unfamiliarity with a more expansive experience. Mind is like space. Fear reflects the gap between the known and the unknown. It points to greater knowledge. Instead of retreating, gently pursue questioning by considering what is necessary or what you would like to see happen. Especially now, do not settle for the familiar answer. Use your imagination to probe further.

New Ways

In our company we encouraged each other to use Questioning Mind in every aspect of the job. It was especially useful in developing responsibility and leadership. For instance, at one point the sales staff realized that we were not bringing in jobs that matched up well with our capacities. A four-color press needs to be used for four-color jobs, preferably using process colors, with medium to long runs. We were not getting enough of this kind of work, which meant that our equipment was not generating the profit it could.

We explored this situation with questions like: "Why? . . . Why not? . . . How else?" The answers that came up helped the sales staff to recognize some underlying fears—fear of not bringing in enough work if we let go of old customers, and of not being able to find new customers. We had chosen unnecessary hardships by taking on and keeping unfit customers. This led to a new round of questions: "How might we begin to look for suitable jobs and the right clients?" Soon it became clear that the process of generating new business works the same way whether you are going after suitable jobs or unsuitable ones. We uncovered a positive, self-motivating incentive to change.

It was distressing to realize how deeply each of us wanted to avoid being blamed when things were going wrong. If we could not find someone else to blame, we would be sure to defend our own position. We would shrug our shoulders, saying, "I did my best," and take refuge in feeling guilty, trying in this way to excuse ourselves from responsibility for correcting the situation. But Questioning Mind took us beyond complacency, fear, and guilt. Like untangling a knot, Questioning Mind unraveled beliefs and assumptions. It restored to awareness the knowledge in what had been unexamined. Released at a subtle level from our positions and defenses, we could take a more creative look at ourselves and the potential of the situation. Reconnecting to our own imagination sparked a desire to work together to do it right.

These were not motivational practices in the usual sense. The questions were not meant to raise morale and pump us up to make a bigger effort. Rather, the answers that evolved over time contained the seeds of new, improved ways of dealing with problems. The solutions were found within the group rather than fed to us from the outside. If Questioning Mind did motivate us, it was because the questions and the answers woke us up, as individuals and as a team.

The fifteen-minute Skillful Means production meetings we held every morning gave us many opportunities to practice Questioning Mind. When a problem came up involving unsuccessful communication, we would ask, "What happened? . . . How did it happen? . . . How else could have happened? . . . What would you have liked to happen? . . . Can you do it that way next time? . . . Do you want to?" With practice we learned that these questions did not require elaborate, explanatory answers. We bypassed reasons, excuses, and the irrelevant to go straight to the missed opportunity. Often new insights came quickly. This led naturally to wanting to take on more responsibilities, so the results next time would be better.

Neutral Openness

Anyone can develop the ability to observe and ask questions. Your caring and your intention to aim for new knowledge protect and direct you. Most of all, use your imagination. A good question is one that opens experience and enables you to see alternative ideas for action. Let go of hidden agendas, preconceived results, or steering in the 'right direction'.

The following exercises may support an open-ended attitude and develop presence of mind. Sitting at your desk or some other comfortable place at work, spend a few moments being aware of your body, moving your awareness from the top of the head down through the trunk, to the base of your spine, and all the way to your feet and hands.

To add to this, when you are walking, take a brief moment to be aware of the movements of your arms and legs in space. If you bring this movement together with your concentration and breath, you may sense a wakefulness with a joyful tinge to it.

To strengthen this state of mind, visualize a column of clear white light in the body, again from the top of the head down o the base of the trunk. Visualize this light as filling the entire body, up and down, without interruptions or blockages, and let it gradually expand outward. Your mind becomes quiet, alert, and stable. With this presence of mind, it is easier to come into the center of the present moment. Remain still, without grasping or pushing away, not sinking down or bubbling up into feelings of elation. When you neither push forward, go backward, nor go down or up, you become neutral and open.

You can use this presence of mind when someone else presents you with an issue or problem. Imagine this situation fully, as if you are there. By not relying only on the words, you gain understanding. Because you are not caught in the dynamics, your view remains clear. When you are really 'in' the story, your questions and insights will be to the point. If the person you are listening to comes to a stop, encourage them to continue by asking more questions that help them to ascertain new knowledge.

Your Gift

Every situation has a positive, a negative, and a neutral aspect to it. Skillful Means calls on you to recognize and challenge the negative, take advantage of the neutral, and draw out and strengthen the positive side. What is it that you can offer—your special gift?

Two questions always seem to have positive results. "What would you have liked to see happen?" and "How would you suggest doing it in the future?" These questions invite real knowledge, which is always exciting. If you are the one reporting, you realize that you are able to know, and do know. Next time you will be able to act according to new knowledge. The question "Can you do it?" takes this process one step further. It strengthens this 'coming out': You are on the verge of empowering yourself.

One special form of Questioning Mind at our company was the threefold vision of becoming a first-class business, meeting financial commitments, and practicing Skillful Means. Here are some of the questions we repeatedly asked, any of which could be adapted to fit your situation:

- What are the ingredients of a first-class business?

    How do other first-class businesses operate?

    What knowledge do we lack to let us work the same way?

    How can we get first-class clients?

    What should we offer that is the best for the client and also for us?

    What are our targets for growth?
    What is the critical path to realizing our goals?

- Are we meeting our financial commitments?

    What bills need to be paid by when?

    What are our priorities?

    What should we do right now to make sure we meet them?

    What is our short- and long-term view of success?

    How can we reduce expenses by five percent?

    How can we shape our workforce to be just right?

- How can we set up a regular Skillful Means practice?

    What new, additional responsibility would each of us like to take on?

Questioning Mind is not about getting information or only about coming up with new ideas. Thinking "Oh yes, I know," or "I guess so" will close the gate to new knowledge. You actually need to develop the answer. State the answer clearly. Better still, write down your thoughts. Then you come face to face with what you know. Only when you speak your mind or write the truth as you know it, will you have the chance to realize: "I know more!" By gently going further, you will discover something that you either forgot or thought you did not know.

Articulating questions and giving yourself permission to find creative answers will give you the knowledge you need to run your business. Eventually the process of putting precise questions and generating creative answers dissolves into 'no more questions, no more answers'. Now you know. With that knowledge you take hold of the dynamic of your life and the growth of your business. Every manager, every leader needs to activate such knowledge on a daily basis—to understand how a situation arises, how it is likely to develop in the future, what opportunities it presents, and how to deal with changes. Can you do it?

10

Meditation:
Just Being

The secret of meditation is
to not cling to what comes to mind.

All great spiritual traditions include some form of meditation, and Tibetan Buddhism is no exception to this rule. In Skillful Means, too, meditation is vital. But unlike traditional approaches, Skillful Means emphasizes practicing meditation while working. Business, with its demand for sharpness and clarity, its focus on time, its bottom-line mentality, and its recognition that knowledge leads to success, is a natural place to meditate. The ingredients needed for a successful undertaking—an undivided mind expansive in time and space—are similar to those that meditation both calls for and develops.

One way to think of meditation is as integration. So often we think one thing, feel another, and act differently altogether; our body and mind are not integrated.

Meditation integrates mind and body, feeling and thinking. It promotes sensing the smaller and the greater at the same time. In business terms this means that we learn to be aware of details in a larger context—each step in the process, as well as the progression as a whole. Meditation enables us to see into time.

As we develop understanding of how to exercise awareness, concentration, and energy, the mind and the body naturally act in harmony. This wholeness is vital to meditation. What was separate is restored to unity.

Beginning Meditation

In everyday life, the functioning of the mind is often reduced to a flow of mental events. Thoughts, images, and sensations all follow one another in rapid succession. As the mind reacts to all this, it tends to become fragmented. Meditation is the remedy to this fragmentation.

If you want to develop wholeness and integrate it into your work, the first step is to recognize how scattered the mind usually is. Now you think one thing, and seemingly without transition you think something else. You 'change your mind' as a new event demands your attention. As you identify with whatever comes to mind, you become the victim of each emotion, each memory or feeling or restless thought. Clinging to the content of the thought, you fall away from the wholeness of experience into small, limited perspectives. As mental activity shifts, your attachment to it makes the mind follow like a shadow. In this state very little counts except: "I want," "I don't want," or "I don't care." You become fundamentally unstable and restless.

To begin to deal with this unsatisfactory pattern, Tarthang Tulku suggests developing relaxation, specifically through activating the flow of feeling in the body. When the mind begins to relax its tight grip on each new thought or image, it becomes open and spacious. You can see more clearly how grasping at thoughts limits and constricts your way of being, setting up a basic lack of awareness.

Another approach to relaxing the attachment to thoughts is to let thoughts and emotions pass through the mind without clinging to them; like visitors, they simply pass through your home without leaving anything behind. Learning to focus on the mind and recognize the stream of mental events without getting lost in it takes practice over time and requires steady discipline. It is possible to learn to let go, gently releasing the tendency to feed thoughts, ideas, concepts, and opinions. Little by little, restlessness diminishes, and the wholeness of experience is restored. As you begin to recapture what had been excluded, you sense that there is more to experience than merely thinking.

In daily life this learning process can be supported by making an effort to 'catch' thoughts that endlessly repeat themselves and let them go. See what happens when you let go of the need to have an opinion, or give up on the urge to repeat over and over what is on your mind. Try focusing instead on what you are doing, or on the big picture. This process of relaxation and focusing does not mean you need to suppress anything. The aim is to pay close attention to the patterns of distraction and the basic restlessness of the mind, with the intention not to continue them. Thoughts exist only for as long as you think them. If they do not receive attention, they will vanish without a trace.

As your thoughts relax in meditation, the mind becomes quiet and receptive. With relaxation you can develop calmness; the mind becomes like a clear, still pond. By itself, a calm mind may merely reflect a state of friendly numbness—not doing any harm, but not of much use either. But calmness cultivates presence of mind, so that clarity can emerge. Body and mind come to life in a balanced and harmonious way. The release of tension fills you with an expanding and deepening aliveness. Being relaxed and calm, you feel at ease, even in the midst of a tense situation. This promotes clarity. The resulting sense of relief helps you to relax even further.

It is also possible to develop calmness and clarity simultaneously. When you observe and question your experience, you gain a greater understanding that frees the mind of what is irrelevant and makes your ways of acting more peaceful. Supporting each other, the qualities of calmness and clarity will open the gates to the exploration of being and doing. By freeing the mind from the stories it is forever telling itself, from its countless excuses and alibis, calmness and clarity start you on the path toward what Tarthang Tulku has called knowledge of freedom.

Beyond these basics, there are many different kinds of meditation practice. In most cases the idea is to give the mind a wholesome new job to do, turning it away from the ordinary routine of thoughts and reactions. With the opening of mind, knowledge and understanding arise naturally.

Meditating While Working

As integration in time and space, meditating requires total involvement—your full energy, your entire mind. It is as if your whole being embraces your activities.

Working well demands the same kind of complete engagement, and so it is natural for work to become meditation. Business in particular, with its need for promptness, follow-up and follow-through, offers an opportunity to deepen meditative awareness. Meeting deadlines, paying the bills, surviving and thriving as a business require that you be fully present and alert. Such presence contacts the dynamic energy of time, and counters tendencies such as hope and fear, doubt and hesitation.

Just like any other company, ours faced a daily challenge in uniting the needs of the clients, the demands of the production flow, the capacity and maintenance needs of equipment, and the capabilities and aspirations of the employees. There was no perfect recipe for success. Practicing meditation while working let us meet these challenges by activating our creative forces over and over. For instance, when one of our sales people would work on making a sale, meditative awareness meant anticipating not only closing the deal, but also the actual production, follow-up, delivery, invoicing, payment, and client and vendor relations—not just now, but in the past, present, and future.

When we meditated in this way on a regular basis, the effects were obvious. We were more stable in our attitudes and attention, and more consistent in our output. We had a greater ability to anticipate problems and needs. When a problem occurred there was no panic, no sense of yet another fire to extinguish. Everyone exhibited clarity about whatever had gone wrong, and an immediate willingness to fix it. It became obvious that it was always best to face trouble sooner, since later it would only have gained in magnitude.

Inner Work

To cultivate meditative awareness in your work, you can imagine your whole being embracing all your activities. This will help you to recognize entanglements as they start to take form and face up to them right away, without getting caught in their web. It helps to imagine being three years further along in time, looking back at the particular situation you are facing now. In the blink of an eye, this expanded time will provide more space, and the problem will appear like a tiny speck. This way you avoid being trapped in repetitive reactions.

You can train yourself to spot problems with open eyes and ears, as if you could see and hear with your entire being. Your senses become wide awake, allowing intuition to inform you. The problem might be anything—a blockage in production, a mix-up with a client, or a concern among your co-workers that has not yet come to the surface. Facing the issue squarely may itself be enough to eliminate it. Many times you do not have to take drastic steps. As soon as the present situation is questioned, it will start to shift. Asking simple, straightforward questions will let you cut to the chase, awakening hidden knowledge: "Why? . . . How? . . .Why not? How else? . . . What do you need? . . . Is it possible?"

A more general approach is to analyze the way you use the mind as you work. For a while, try working without any fixations or expectations. Aim to make things lighter in every way. Observe the mind's tendency to mutter complaints or judgments, such as, "Oh no, not again!" Note how these mental patterns freeze your creativity, binding your energy to concepts and labels.

You can deepen the quality of meditation while you work by deepening relaxation. In the midst of commotion, are you able to let go? Can you relax into the tension? Is the breath gentle, even? Do you spot sensations or feelings in the body that might bring a wider awareness? If you make a habit of asking these questions on the job, some of the tension will melt away, turning into pure energy. Then you can focus on what is happening and what is really important, without being dependent on the 'doings' of the mind.

In order to develop relaxation while working, it is important to feel the experience, whatever it is. Contacting the sensations in the body or the 'feel' of a situation keeps you anchored in the present. Similarly, by listening to the sounds of machines and voices, you will develop a new understanding of how equipment works and how other people's minds function. You will be able to sense what your co-workers have in mind and how to relate to them. You can anticipate opportunities and will know how to deal with predicaments.

The easiest way to develop meditation at work is by bringing awareness to time. As your concentration develops, there will be a merging of energy, awareness, and time. Working and being in time become inseparable. You will be more grounded in your work, sustained by a sense of stability and balance. Distractions that waste time and energy will simply be unacceptable. As the mind becomes efficient, each movement and each action has a purpose, and energy and time appear to be in plentiful supply.

Relaxation and awareness of time go hand in hand. We are convinced that time is moving, but is our experience moving too? Relaxing into what you are doing enables you to experience ever smaller units of time, until eventually there are no gaps in awareness and time. You can go beyond the duality of past and future, arriving at a timeless and open sort of time that is the heart of direct experience.

Practicing meditation while you work helps to integrate the body, breath, and mind. The mind grows steady, making you feel lighter and more alert. With integration comes inner integrity, which will show in the way you work: You act with confidence and conviction, the quality of your work is dependable, and you fulfill your promises.

Discovering Mind

Your well-being and your accomplishments depend on how well you understand and train the mind. With awareness of mind you recognize how the habit of labeling the content of mental activity tends to disconnect you from immediate experience. This 'doing' of the mind cuts you off from directly experiencing the interaction of inner and outer through the senses. Events go by in a blur, and only much later, when the mind's activity has settled down, do you even realize what you were feeling or sensing at the time.

Developing meditative awareness at work allows you to contact, communicate with, and digest the feeling tones of experience. You become aware of the ongoing background of your experience, a continuum 'below' or 'behind' internal dialogues. Awareness of this foundation for experience allows you to integrate awareness and time in the body.

When awareness, concentration, and energy join forces with the insights into the workings of the mind that meditation offers, work is transformed. Without attaching itself to one particular way of doing or one specific way of being, the mind remains loose, crisp, and clear. Paying attention to the feel of working and the background of experience, you can bypass 'complaining mind' completely, or at least refuse to let it continue.

Uniting meditation and work is a challenging practice. You will have to train and exercise the mind, and this training will not always be easy. You may be disheartened now and then, or get off-balance by allowing elation at your progress to disrupt your awareness. Habits of distraction will often tempt you. Yet when you stay with it, meditating at work becomes a constructive habit, something to cherish, even long for.

Learn to encourage yourself. If you lose focus, return to it time and again. The quicker you take up meditating again, the deeper meditation becomes. You are teaching the mind to remain open, and this will eventually make you stronger. Just continue massaging and cultivating the mind. Open up intellectual speculation, judgments, and the mind's doings. Then the experience of working becomes deeper and vaster. Being fully engaged in each situation you are in, extending yourself in time and space, you begin to act in ways that are suitable now and for the future.

Using Obstacles

Many texts in the Tibetan tradition point out that the main obstacles to meditation are laziness, excitement, and forgetting the instructions. The path of meditation may be nothing other than the ongoing practice of overcoming these hurdles to integration.Until we overcome the obstacles we encounter, we carry within us and are constantly generating the seeds of potential new obstacles.

Getting results in meditation is in many ways similar to succeeding in business. It all amounts to finding first-rate solutions to problems, a fundamentally constructive approach. Instead of viewing an obstacle as some kind of failure, look at it as a hindrance that will recur again as long as you fail to deal with it. Seen in this way, dealing with obstacles is the best way of making progress, both for you individually and for your company. The strength, endurance, and creativity you develop by taking on each new difficulty become your refuge; there is no place for despondency. As awareness opens, new worlds with more opportunities emerge, and energy is released for creative accomplishments.

Progress

Signs of progress in meditation do not always manifest themselves in obvious ways. Experiences or reactions that you find discouraging may actually be a sign of improvement, for they make the working of the mind visible. For example, a rising restlessness that annoys and discourages you might well indicate an impending transition to greater awareness. If in the face of it, you can remain still and focused, restlessness may yield to openness, ease, and an inner feeling of gentleness. On the other hand, a state of mind that is superficially pleasant and soothing may be anything but clear; it may drift subtly into a kind of sleep that may be calm, but seems as if nobody is home.

**Ten-Week Program for
Beginning to Meditate While Working**

Week One   Be aware of your posture while you sit
and your movements while you walk.

Week Two   Listen to others.
Try to understand without relying
only on words.
Be receptive to the whole being of the
other person.

Week Three   Let go of the need to have opinions.

Week Four   Accept without blame and work with
what there is.

Week Five   Work with no fixations and no
expectations.

Week Six   Be aware of the beginning, middle,
and end of each project and each day.

Week Seven   Be aware moment to moment,
with no gaps in awareness of time

Week Eight   Always bear in mind what is good for
the company.

Week Nine   Find positive solutions and make
decisions.

Week Ten   Notice the feel of each situation.
Make everything lighter.

As meditation develops, however, there will be signs of progress you can rely upon. These include a sense of joy, a poised alertness, and the feeling that you are working well. From time to time, you realize that your experience is no longer fragmented. The work is doing itself. You are 'just being'. You are meditating!

11

Quality on Time

The more we challenge ourselves in our work,
the more we will enjoy what we do and
the more we willl have to offer.

Working wholeheartedly and effectively is ultimately a matter of 'just being'—being authenti-
cally creative and awake in time and space. When you
are at ease and at the same time entirely engaged in
what you are doing, the aliveness of the experience of
working is guaranteed. Then you make everything
lighter and to the point.

Skillful Means offers myriad ways to realize this
transformation, all revolving around activating knowledge. Making your work a path of knowledge can rev-
olutionize your life, and help stabilize the growth of
any enterprise. Your first steps on this path will give you
a glimpse of new horizons; there is so much more to
know, and access to this knowledge is possible. Any
entrepreneur starts with a vision—the seed of what is

possible. Activating knowledge and acting on it inspires this vision and keeps it alive.

The spirit of the individual and the soul of the company both hinge on putting knowledge into action. In
the end it all comes down to what you do with your time
and how you do it—to making the most and the best of
time. You can begin by focusing on getting the most
positive accomplishments from your work. As this
process is put into motion, it becomes increasingly evident how to improve and expand; it is as if knowledge
informs you through your actions, without your having
to apply any special techniques.

The knowledge that shapes the art of living and
working is about time and quality. Both the individual
and the company thrive on using time well and realizing top quality.

When time and quality are its foundation, a growing business will be strong and stable. The needs and
aspirations of every individual will naturally be met,
and it will be easy to service the clients, bring vitality to
individual employees, and fulfill the goals of the company. The pillars of time and quality are communication, cooperation, and responsibility. Awareness of any
of these three factors will instantly have positive effects,
circulating throughout the company to influence employees, clients, and suppliers.

The employees and the enterprise share a common
ground in their wish for quality and time. What productivity, efficiency, and profit are for the company,
are happiness, well-being, and a life worth living in the

eyes of the worker. It is merely a difference in terminology. In fact they share another desire: Both want their lives to be a success; they want to act efficiently without wasting opportunities, and most of all to earn a return on their investment of time.

Being born is like receiving a supply of gold bars, one for each year of your life. You may invest this vast wealth or you may neglect to use it, but whatever you do, every year a bar of gold will be taken away from you. Would you not like to see a return on your investment? Are not all human beings looking for an annual profit from what they do with each year, each day of their lives?

Success Story

There seems to be a general tendency for the goals of the company and the aspirations of the individual employees to grow apart. More often than not, this division is mirrored in the structure of the company. The organization splits up internally, with management on one side and employees on the other. There may be a similar separation between two departments, between two co-workers, or even within one person who makes a strong distinction between work and free time.

When these structures take hold, divisiveness grows and festers. The 'whole' moves toward disintegration, and the rift that forms can seem insurmountable. For the company, this is a precarious situation: When people place their energy and hope outside the business, productivity and profit are at risk. The individual will simply feel that the time spent at work is wasted.

Sensing this loss of commonality, a management strategy may be to 'get on the same page', ensuring that everyone is of one mind and dedicated to a plan for unified execution. This may be effective for the moment. But why not go further? Instead of just being on the same page, why not write the entire book together? One plot, with one central theme—quality on time. This theme will resonate in all the endeavors of the company. If each person plays a unique and necessary part, the story will be a success story. This way of 'creating uniqueness in the whole' nurtures the dignity of the individual and the solidity of the company. In each undertaking, this is the pillar of creativity.

Just as the company aims for daily activity that is productive, so the individual wishes to lead a productive life. Since any worker who is young at heart will naturally want to learn rather than stay 'on hold', the interest of the company and the need of the worker are identical. The goals of the company can best be realized by refining the inner resources of the individual. This will mean more efficiency for the company, and enjoyment in work for the employee. To be content with a day's work is like making profit or increasing the value of each shareholder's stock. In both cases, the aim is satisfaction.

The Best of Time

To achieve the highest quality of time in work and in life you need stable energy, strong concentration, and awareness that is simultaneously sharp and expansive.

Time & Quality

For the Organization	*For the Individual*
productivity	skills
efficiency	joy
profit	satisfaction
meeting goals	meaningfulness
using resources	developing potential
expanding	refining inner resources
success	inner growth

As you refine these resources you will be able to make the best of your abilities. Your purpose strengthens, and any sense of frustration you might feel diminishes or even disappears.

It is best to cultivate your inner resources by developing them in relation to time. Connecting awareness to time will turn around any undertaking. Touched by awareness, time expands, and you start to appreciate and capture the value of each moment. It is like being aware of the day as it unfolds—the sun rising, reaching its peak at midday, and setting in the evening. This progression not only represents a day in your life, but also symbolizes the cycle of beginning, middle, and end of a project—or a lifetime. When you connect with their urgency, time and light will prove a most reliable refuge.

At our company we practiced five trainings for promoting awareness of time and making things lighter.

We called them: How to Open, How to Care, How to Protect, How to Energize, and How to Accomplish. To explore these links and their benefit for yourself, you may experiment with each topic for a week at a time, or preferably for a month.

How to Open focuses on time and the six senses. Awakening and developing sensitivity to the nature and dynamic of time enlarges the sense of space. Here, in the midst of perpetual change, there is stability in the flow of time. As you become attuned to the coming and going of each moment, and the beginning and end of moment after moment, you quietly settle into change, instead of fighting it.

Encouraging yourself not to be fixed or close-minded, you can practice open communication with yourself and others. In doing this, you will sense the power of thoughts, and realize that both the mind and ways of working are intrinsically open. With patience you may learn to change the way you work. Enjoying the sense of openness, you become at ease in the feeling of freedom.

How to Care becomes natural once you have begun with 'how to open'. It is the heart of these five trainings. Through caring the quality of your knowledge and intuition improve. Learning to care and taking responsibility have a positive impact on both you personally and the organization as a whole.

To practice caring, look around for reflections of indifference. You will find that when you do practice caring—for instance by cleaning up or making something better—the effects will be visible right away. The other side of this practice is to encourage yourself to observe any lack of caring that makes you want to hide or to hold on to resentment. Aversion makes it impossible to connect to the work or to other people. Turn it around little by little by experimenting with generosity, with simple gestures of caring: a word, a glance, an act of recognition or appreciation. Then time will offer you a glimpse of its generosity, inviting you to care from moment to moment.

How to Protect evolves around the quality of your work and the quality of your product or service. Acknowledge that in every action, the individual and the company are at stake. Take to heart what you value. With discipline you will learn to recognize and guard against undermining influences. In a nutshell, 'how to protect' is about knowledge of the positive. The desire to protect what has meaning becomes like an armor, giving you confidence to face any challenge.

At our company it seemed that each activity, every gesture was asking for protection. The financial and legal commitments, the safety and inspiration of the workers, the production, the quality and service, the clients, and even the company's name—everything called for care, protection. Sometimes out of fear, at other times out of love, we focused intensively on 'how to protect'.

How to Energize can be understood by observing your level of energy. By connecting with awareness and with the gut, energy will be prevented from draining away. You will discover that with a little effort it is possible to get a grip on your vitality. Learning to energize becomes a self-motivating force.

Working with deadlines is a powerful and effective way to become familiar with your own energy and experience the momentum that builds when everyone cooperates. The energy that fuels success is not always comfortable: Alertness and involvement in work are sometimes fueled by the energy of fear and anxiety as well as by appreciation. So do not wait for the clients' demands, but instead set deadlines for yourself and for the company. In this way you stimulate participation and bring splendor to your work.

How to Accomplish needs a structure. An accomplishment does not come about by random acts. Make a clear outline, a critical path in your own mind about what you wish to concentrate on—at this meeting, on this day, for this month. This invites planning and a course of action. Clarifying your short- and long-term motivation and goals will naturally strengthen your accomplishments. You will discover that it is not necessary to map out every detail.

As the plan of action takes shape, the best thing to do is to begin, to just start getting results. The energy of doing develops knowledge as you go along. To bolster future achievements, take time to recognize, appreciate, and evaluate the results you get. They provide the feedback necessary for knowledge, and the fuel for the joy of working. The glow of satisfaction that accompanies accomplishments becomes a light that illuminates future endeavors and inspires faith in what is possible.

Being on a Mission

You have a mission, as an individual and as part of a business. Once in a while take the time to remind yourself what this mission is. Give yourself some space and time to review your goals and accomplishments. Determine what is important for the future; refresh your commitment. It is tempting to focus on what is easy or on what you do best, but challenging your abilities is an adventure. If obstacles discourage you, how can you rekindle your love for life and for your work? Create some time for internal nourishment. Even if you think you know the answer, ask yourself anew: "What do I want to get out of life?" If your life were coming to an end and you were looking back upon your past, what has made life worth living?

Your mission in life is a journey in time. Time is like breath, the flow of life. If the connection to time is lost, laziness takes over and your involvement spirals down into mediocrity and decay. Consciously drawing out what is possible links your body and mind, as well as the total operation of your business, to time. When you connect to the urgency of time, every day and every moment become a possibility for quality time.

Develop this link to time through refining your inner resources—awareness, concentration, and energy. Let the power of your potential be an inspiration to you. Your abilities are like diamonds in the rough: You can continually heat, cut, and polish them. The more you cultivate your energy and intelligence, the more you stabilize your strengths and transform your weaknesses into supporters of the goals you cherish.

At our company, we developed a simple map that ties the resources of body and mind to the three key elements of time. The aim is to bring action and quality to increasingly higher levels of success, based on dissecting time into 'What', 'When', and 'How'. This map is unique in that both the company and the individual can focus on the same thing, simultaneously.

Challenge Your Abilities, by focusing on:

	What	When	How
Body/ workforce	skills productivity	joy efficiency	satisfaction benefits
Breath/ flow	Awakening Time in-output	Control Time dependable	Mastering Time creative
Mind/ quality	commitment profit	appreciation opportunities	art of working MasterWork

---

Work for a week with one block at a time. Start with block one: Challenge your skills and the productivity of the company. Record progress and results, quantifying everything in numbers and graphs. Can you imagine your energy connecting with the energy of productivity? It will be evident that improving all kinds of skills will affect the level of production, your own and that of the company. What is needed to increase accomplishments? Can you begin to *do* that?

As your training progresses, move through each block in turn. When you work with the two topics in block 'commitment-profit', for instance, challenge your power to choose, and strengthen your commitment. How will doing this affect the profit or benefit of what you do? Note that increasing profit depends primarily on the commitment of everyone involved.

Ultimately, you refine the art of working by challenging your abilities in relation to time. If you commit to cultivating your abilities in time, the preciousness of time shines through in all you do. Being focused on what you do, when you act, and how you work brings a touch of pride to everything you undertake. This way of working keeps your feet on the ground and your head high. You enter the domain of MasterWork. Success in life and work comes effortlessly, informed by caring and love.

The workforce at Dharma Enterprises was composed in equal numbers of women and men, and the readers will also be both female and male. It would have been right to use "he or she" when addressing them. For the sake of readability however, I chose the side of convention, opting for "he" and "him" throughout the entire book, although I am aware of the unjustness of this choice.

Appendix

Epigraphs and quotes by Tarthang Tulku, unless otherwise noted. All books published by Dharma Publishing.

Introduction: *Knowledge of Freedom*, p. xii; *TNMC Annals*, Vol. 5, p. v (Padmasambhava); *Gesture of Balance*, p. 25; *Skillful Means*, p. xx.

Chapter 1: *Mastering Successful Work*, p. 95.

Chapter 2: *Mastering Successful Work*, p. 7.

Chapter 3: *Mastering Successful Work*, p. 7.

Chapter 4: *Mastering Successful Work*, pp. 233–234.
For the Paramitas–*Kindly Bent to Ease Us* (Longchenpa) pp. 67–68

Chapter 5: *Mastering Successful Work*, pp. 199–200.

Chapter 6: *Skillful Means*, pp. 116–117.

Chapter 7: *Knowledge of Freedom*, p. 368.

Chapter 8: *Mastering Successful Work*, pp. 66, 53.

Chapter 9: *Knowledge of Freedom*, p. 83.

Chapter 10: *Gesture of Balance*, p. 77.

Chapter 11: *Mastering Successful Work*, p. 235.

Index

209

Books by Tarthang Tulku

Skillful Means

Mastering Successful Work

Knowledge of Freedom

Gesture of Balance

Openness Mind

Hidden Mind of Freedom

Kum Nye Relaxation, Parts 1 and 2

Time, Space, and Knowledge

Love of Knowledge

Knowledge of Time and Space

Dynamics of Time and Space

Visions of Knowledge

Sacred Dimensions of Time and Space

Dharma Publishing

2425 Hillside Avenue   Berkeley, California 94704

(510) 548–5407

Dedicated to the Longevity of Tarthang Tulku.

This stupa was built at Dharma Enterprises in 1991, and placed at
the Tibetan Nyingma Institute in Berkeley, California.